Hiking to Siberia

Hiking to Siberia

Curious Tales of Travel and Travelers

Lawrence Millman

sunnyoutside
Buffalo

Acknowledgments

Most of these essays appeared, albeit in somewhat different form, in the *Yukon News*, *Atlantic Monthly*, *Christian Science Monitor*, *Swank*, *Islands*, *Los Angeles Times*, *A Movable Feast* (Lonely Planet), *The Walrus*, and *Arctic*. Of the editors I've worked with, I'd especially like to thank Peter Lesniak, formerly of the *Yukon News*. I'd also like to thank Kathie Hodge for her expert text wrangling and David McNamara for transforming my prose into lo! this little book. A Pearlman Grant underwrote the costs of the Hudson Strait trip described in "The Green Man."

sunnyoutside
PO Box 911
Buffalo, NY 14207
USA

www.sunnyoutside.com

"Soap and education are not as sudden as a massacre,
but they are more deadly in the long run."
—*Mark Twain*

"De-spiritualize yourself: what you cannot
find on earth is not worth seeking."
—*Norman Douglas*

"Pissing in one's shoe keeps no man warm for long."
—*Icelandic Proverb*

Contents

Introduction:
No News Is Good News

LET'S SAY YOU'RE TRAVELING in northeastern Siberia, specifically the region known as Chukotka. At one point, you happen to visit a reindeer camp, where you hear the following conversation between two Chukchi men who haven't seen each other for a while:

"*Napse, dohor?*" one of the men says. "What news, friend?"

"*Napse, napse,*" replies the other man. "I have no news."

"Me, either. Except I ate a few *wapaks* [*Amanita muscaria* mushrooms] two days ago and flew to Uelen."

"Funny I didn't see you there. I did the same thing myself two days ago."

"My visit was short. I had to get back to my reindeer."

"Any news about your reindeer?"

"None. Any news about yours?"

"*Napse.*"

There follows a pause. Tea might be served. Or perhaps vodka. "Well, I do have some news about my reindeer," the first man remarks. "Some of them have a very bad viral infection."

"*Tarsi qlapseq, dohor!* I'm sorry, friend. Have you taken them to the shaman yet?"

"The shaman gave them the infection. He was not pleased that I borrowed his daughter for a few nights."

"Well, I have some news, too. My first-born son has become the new Deputy Governor of Chukotka..."

Such interchanges, which are not unusual among the Chukchi, seem to me an excellent way to convey information: a slow, almost reluctant release rather than the machine gun-like assaults of (for example) the six o'clock news, which tries to squeeze everything—from celebrity divorces to deadly earthquakes, from infants left in dumpsters to tomorrow's overcast skies—into less than half an hour.

In 2004, I did in fact travel in Chukotka, and for the better part of a month, I had virtually no contact with the outside world. If the Bubonic Plague had returned to Europe, or if terrorists had again wreaked havoc on New York City's skyline, I probably wouldn't have known about it.

But what about the Internet? you might ask. After all, it would have brought to everyone's notice a new epidemic almost before that epidemic occurred. True, I'd reply, but I never carry a computer-type device with me on my travels, lest I become tethered to the world I left behind. And even if I did have one of these devices in Chukotka, I was staying in a series of *yurangis*, reindeer-skin dwellings that typically are not equipped with Wi-Fi.

No Wi-Fi? you might exclaim: How awful! But it isn't really all that bad. A Chukchi reindeer herder derives very little benefit from hearing about the trials and tribulations of the world beyond Chukotka. For him, terrorism is when one of his reindeer is stolen. In the past, terrorism was when Stalin collectivized all his reindeer.

I tend not to suffer from news deprivation, either. For the news, to me, is an abstraction. Another way of saying this is that I don't believe Obama, Putin, or Arnold Schwarzenegger really exist until I actually meet them. By contrast, the ground below my feet is genuine, at once hard and wondrous, although in Chukotka that ground is becoming considerably less hard than it once was, thanks to global warming.

One reason I travel is to hear a rather different kind of news from the six o'clock variety: who might have run afoul of the local shaman; what species of birds are singing in the trees; on what type of cuisine former cannibals now dine (answer: often spam, because it reputedly tastes like human flesh); and so on.

Likewise, I travel to escape what Norman Douglas called "the vast perambulating lunatic asylum of civilization" nearly a hundred years ago. I don't think of such escapes as escapism, though. Instead, I'm trying to discover the few remaining places that have not lost their marrow.

During my wanderings in Chukotka, I happened to find myself in the company of an elderly Chukchi man who, over the course of an entire afternoon, allowed only a single newsworthy item to escape his lips. *"Yest' mnogo komarov,"* he told me. "There are lots of mosquitoes."

"Lots," I agreed, slapping at a few.

And then we fell into a silence so perfect that I could even hear the mosquitoes calling my name.

—*Lawrence Millman*
Cambridge, Massachusetts
June 2012

Hiking to Siberia

ONE DAY IN 1927, a thirty-year-old woman walked out of New York City, continued walking to Buffalo, crossed into Canada and then hiked all the way to Hazelton, British Columbia. To any question that came her way, she would reply in a heavy Russian accent: "I go to Siberia."

Wherever she went, this woman—whose anglicized name was Lillian Alling—inspired speculation. "Writes novels or perhaps a criminal," observed one person who met her. Others thought she might be the Russian czar's last daughter returning to her homeland on the cheap. "On the cheap" is at least correct: during much of her journey, Lillian wore a pair of mismatched men's shoes and carried a lightweight shoulder bag that seemed hardly any bigger than a pocketbook. In fact, it may have been a pocketbook. She also carried a wrench for protection against bears as well as men.

The next spring, Lillian set out for the Yukon—the place where I first heard about her. An old prospector named Jack Goulding told me that he'd met her almost seventy years earlier. Or tried to meet her. In response to his offer of help, she frowned at him and just walked on. Hardly anyone paid much attention to her, he told me, because "folks used to walk in those days." Another old-timer disagreed. He said plenty of Yukoners took notice of Lillian because, as he put it, "she was completely wacky." His evidence for this: she was a woman traveling alone.

The more I heard about Lillian, the more intrigued I became, and at last I decided to write a book about her journey, which struck me as being both remarkable and "wacky." To cite just one example: she hiked the entire 330 miles of the Yukon Telegraph Trail, a formidable slog for an experienced hiker, but several notches above formidable for a lone woman seemingly unequipped for anything more daunting than a stroll in an urban park. That this woman does not look particularly robust in the few known photographs of her makes her achievement all the more remarkable, or perhaps all the more wacky.

For my book, I decided to follow in Lillian's footsteps wherever possible, so I set out to hike at least a portion of the Yukon Telegraph Trail myself. Unfortunately, it was no longer a trail by this time, and I soon found myself plodding through a boreal hell composed of muskeg, virtually impenetrable undergrowth, and devil's club, a plant armed with cat-claw spines. I was under constant assault by horse flies and mosquitoes, which seemed to work in tandem with each other. Here and there I saw skeins of old telegraph wire, and at one point I encountered a moose skeleton wrapped in wire like a mummy. The poor animal had gotten tangled up in the wire, and in trying to escape, had gotten even more tangled up in it, dying, I could only hope, quickly.

After five very unpleasant days, I gave up. But Lillian did not give up. She hiked on, sometimes staying with the telegraph linemen, who fed and clothed her, and in one instance, even died for her. Scotty Ogilvie was scouting out the trail for her when he slipped and fell into the Ningunsaw River. Due to heavy rains, the river was raging, and he ended up drowning. A short while later, the river returned to its former low level. Seeing it at this level, Lillian said: "How can a man drown in a dry creek? He must have been very stupid."

A thoughtless remark, but hardly a surprising one. For Lillian had only one thing on her mind, and that was her journey. Human sympathy had no place in this journey, nor did humans themselves. When she reached Atlin, a town at the end of the telegraph trail, she was carrying the hide of a dog stuffed with grass. One of the lineman had given her a Tahltan bear dog as a pack animal. Somehow the dog had died, and Lillian stuffed it. "He's my only friend, and he'll always be with me," she remarked of the dog.

A preference for stuffed animals over unstuffed people suggests that her emotional development may have been somewhat stunted. A Tlingit woman in Atlin more or less confirmed this for me. As a young girl, she had met Lillian when the solitary hiker was passing through town.

"What did she say?" I asked excitedly.

"Oh, she didn't say anything," the woman told me. "She just sat down and played dolls with me."

Lillian's journey took her to the Yukon town of Whitehorse, where she spent the night of August 28, 1928 in a cheap hotel. The next day, she began walking to Dawson City, with only a small loaf of bread for the 325-mile trip. By now, the territory's newspapers were posting brief articles about the person they called "The Mystery Woman." On October 5, she reached Dawson, where she decided to spend the winter. Shortly after she arrived, she got a job as a domestic servant at St. Paul's, a church-run hostel for orphan and part-Native children.

In 2002, I located a ninety-five-year-old nun who'd worked with Lillian at St. Paul's, and I asked her what she remembered about the so-called Mystery Woman. Sister Anne-Marie paused for a moment, then said: "She was always stealing sugar from the hospital pantry."

A typically Russian obsession with sweets? Fuel for the haul to Siberia? Or simply a kleptomaniac urge? The elderly nun did not know, nor could she even hazard a guess, although she did tell me that Lillian was "a troubled soul."

In the spring of 1929, Lillian bought a rowboat with her hospital earnings, put it in the Yukon River, and began paddling west toward Alaska. A local journalist who'd been tailing her noted that she didn't seem to know anything about boats, even how to paddle them.

As it heads in a westerly direction from Dawson, the Yukon's current is relatively gentle, usually no more than five or six knots, so a person without any knowledge of boats could just go with the proverbial flow and probably end up in western Alaska. But no one living on the river reported a small boat with a woman in it during the spring or summer of 1929. That summer a woman did drown in the river not far from Eagle, Alaska, but she was a Native, and she'd probably committed suicide.

Could Lillian might have encountered another solitary, William Yanert, in his hermitage of Purgatory on the Yukon River? Yanert put scary-looking sculptures around his cabin to scare off potential visitors; he composed his own gravestone epitaph, the last line of which reads "Mush off, and let me be." If he and Lillian had indeed met, they probably would have frowned at each other, and then gone their respective ways, he to constructing his gargoyles and she to her paddling.

Later in the same year a Yupik Eskimo man reputedly saw a white woman pushing a two-wheeled cart along the beach near Wales, an Alaskan village situated on the Bering Strait and the closest spot in North America to Siberia. The cart in question had a stuffed dog lying on top of it...or so the story goes.

As I was pondering what I would do with so many "reputedlys" and "probablys," a friend in Whitehorse suggested that I turn Lillian's journey into a novel. Maybe she was pursuing a lover, or the husband who'd abandoned her, to the Yukon goldfields. Or maybe I could turn her into a female version of Chris McCandless, the hero of *Into the Wild*, except that I shouldn't be too obvious about it—i.e., I shouldn't let her go near a schoolbus.

Here I might add that novelist Amy Bloom did turn Lillian into a fictional character several years ago. In her bestseller *Away*, she named this character Lillian Leyb, although Ms. Bloom does not acknowledge (shame!) the fact that her Lillian is based on a real-life Lillian. For my part, I had no desire to fictionalize a person who seemed to me like fiction already. Likewise, I figured my persistence would pay off sooner or later. I also figured that if I got a book contract, I could finance a trip to the Alaskan and Siberian sides of the Bering Strait, where a bit of sleuthing would help me discover Lillian's fate.

The editor who'd worked on my previous book was not enthused about the idea. "What if you don't get any more material?" he said. "Readers don't want to be left with question marks, nor do they want to be left in the dark about whether the person they've been following for several hundred pages made it to her destination."

"Well, there's some anecdotal evidence that she did make it," I told him.

Which was true. In 1965, a Californian named Arthur Elmore visited a Russian friend of his who'd spent his boyhood in the Siberian town of Provideniya. As they were reminiscing, the friend recalled an incident from around the year 1930. One afternoon he was walking near the town's harbor, and he saw the police interrogating a very worn-looking Caucasian woman. The woman was with three Alaska Yupik men who had transported her across the Bering Strait in a skin boat. Eventually, the police led all four away.

"According to the story, the woman knelt down and kissed the ground once she got out of the skin boat," I said.

"Is Arthur Elmore still alive?" the editor asked me.

"Google doesn't seem to think so," I said.

"The story's just too vague. We don't even know if the woman in Provideniya was your mystery woman, or what became of her after the police hauled her off."

Not long after we'd had this conversation, a nonfiction book about Lillian Alling was in fact published. Or I should say that *The Woman Who Walked to Russia* tries hard to be about Lillian, but the author, an Australian writer with the extremely writerly name of Cassandra Pybus, keeps running into dead ends. A few pages before the end of the book, seemingly desperate, she proposes that Lillian must have been pursuing a mate. There could have been no other explanation for her marathon trek, Ms. Pybus concludes.

I could think of several other explanations, but it didn't matter, since I was getting frustrated by dead ends myself. Then just as I was about to jettison the idea of a book, I got a job as a lecturer on a cruise ship whose itinerary included, among other Siberian ports of call, Provideniya. Suddenly my interest in Lillian Alling was revived. I imagined myself meeting an elderly man in Provideniya and having him tell me something like this: "Dear Lillian! She was a bit odd, but we had many good times together..."

What I did discover in Provideniya turned out to be nearly as good. In return for an extra lecture or two, the cruise's expedition leader allowed me to do some exploring on my own around the town. I wandered among picturesque *izbas* (log cabins), dined on whale blubber and salmon eggs with a Chukchi man, and at last ended up in a cemetery that looked like it hadn't been tended in quite some time. Having a knowledge of Russian, I began reading some of the more legible inscriptions on the gravestones. All at once I read these words:

LILLIA LVOVNA ALLING

Scarcely able to contain my excitement, I cleared away a bit of lichen, and then read the following words:

KONETS PUTEE

Konets Putee means "Here the Journey Ends." At last—a significant clue in my attempt to solve the mystery woman's mystery! With trembling hand, I reached for my camera and began photographing the inscription.

Actually, I did no such thing. For between ushering the passengers on and off the ship, on and off the town's only bus, in and out of the town's museum, and away from locals trying to hawk Lenin medals, I didn't read any revealing inscription on a gravestone or even visit a cemetery. Nor did I see a single picturesque log cabin anywhere in the town, for Provideniya consisted almost exclusively of Soviet-era block housing whose architectural model appears to have been Hitler's bunker.

If the truth is at once stranger and more elusive than fiction, it can also be quite a bit more mundane. Lillian Alling never seemed to understand why anyone would be interested in her journey. In all probability, she was just going home.

An Icelandic Snake Story

THE ROADS IN ICELAND'S Westfjords are awful even for a country that seems to pride itself on the awfulness of its roads: they consist mostly of gravel, potholes, and corrugated ridges, with the odd boulder tossed in for good measure.

I was once hitchhiking in the Westfjords when I heard what I thought was a telltale crunching sound in the distance. Uh-oh, an avalanche, I thought. But the crunching got nearer, and then a battered old Volvo pulled up alongside me. Inside the car was a lean, almost cadaverous man whose hair stuck up from his head like lengths of 13-amp fuse wire. "Where are you going?" he asked me.

"To Latrabjorg," I replied.

"Ah, you want to see the famous bird cliffs. Hop in, and I will take you there."

I threw my rucksack into the back seat and climbed in beside him. As we drove along, he was silent. He seemed to be brooding over some dark, typically Nordic issue. At last he said: "I will tell you a story about my own travels."

Ten years ago he had sailed down to Caracas, Venezuela, as a deck-hand on a Danish freighter. He'd planned to sail back to Copenhagen on the same freighter, but the man sitting next to him in a Caracas bar made him change his mind.

"Diamonds," this man, a Venezuelan prospector, told him. "Diamonds as big as your eyeballs, señor. You will find them in a place called El Mundo Perdido."

The prospector reached into his shirt pocket and brought out a huge diamond.

In a very short time, my driver was heading to the El Mundo Perdido district with some packhorses and a half-breed guide named Jorge. Once there, he set up camp, whereupon he and Jorge proceeded to jab their picks into likely looking rocks.

Meanwhile, he kept seeing a bushmaster. Wherever he went, around his camp or down by the river, the snake seemed to be watching him with its tiny pellet eyes. It always managed to elude the blade of his machete.

"It is no ordinary snake, señor," Jorge told him, "but a shape-shifter or perhaps a demon."

One evening when he went down to the river to collect some water, he stepped on the bushmaster. If his trousers had been loose, he would have been safe, but his trousers were clinging to his sweaty legs, and the snake's fangs entered his thigh just above the knee. The pain was excruciating.

Jorge flung him over one of the packhorses and took him fifty miles to the clinic at Santa Elena. By the time they arrived, the poison had infected his whole leg.

"If the bone is black," the clinic's German doctor told him, "your leg will have to come off."

He put in his drill. The bone was black.

"Tomorrow," the doctor announced, "I will amputate."

The next day there were some emergencies—an Indian girl's appendectomy, an Indian who'd been knifed in the chest—that kept the doctor busy. The day after that, the drill came up white.

"You are a lucky man," the doctor observed. "I have nine legs in my collection. Yours would have been the tenth..."

So, apparently, the story ended. My driver did not say another word until we reached Latrabjorg. I thanked him for the lift and started to get out of the car, but his fingers grasped the sleeve of my anorak.

"Wait," he said, "you must hear the rest."

Once his leg had healed, he told me, he'd flown back to Iceland. Shortly after he'd returned to the Westfjords, he was gathering driftwood when he noticed a large black snake coiled up on the beach. It was, in fact, a bushmaster. The same bushmaster that had bitten him.

"But there are no snakes in Iceland," I protested.

"You are wrong, my friend," he said. "There is at least one snake—the snake from El Mundo Perdido. I see it everywhere..."

Then he drove off.

A day or so later, I was hitchhiking between Latrabjorg and Patreksfjordur when I heard a familiar crunching noise, and the same Volvo pulled up alongside me. This time a more robust man was seated behind the wheel.

"Hop in," the man said to me, opening the door.

As we rumbled along, I asked my driver if this car belonged to him. I told him that I'd seen it or an exact replica of it on the road not too long ago.

"It must have been another car," he replied. "For this wreck is mine. I inherited it from my brother after he died in a South American hospital."

"How did your brother die?" I inquired a bit uneasily.

"He was bitten by some kind of poisonous snake. They amputated his leg, but it was too late."

A chill went up and down my spine, and I asked the man to stop the car.

"You want to enjoy the view?" he smiled, rolling to a halt.

"No," I told him. "I've decided to walk for a while. Maybe get some fresh air. Thanks for the lift."

After I got out of the car, I tried to think of some rational explanation for what had happened, but I kept coming back to the fact that I'd gotten a lift from a dead man. I bent over and vomited by the side of the road.

In Patreksfjordur, I learned the truth: that the two men who'd given me lifts were local farmers who—perhaps as a respite from long hours spent with sheep—made a practice of conning visitors. They would take a visitor to a pile of glacial debris, remove their hats, and solemnly say, "This is the grave of the Norse god Thor." Or they would claim that many Icelanders had igloos inside their houses, and that they used those igloos as their bedrooms.

Sometimes, too, they would tell hitchhikers about their island's solitary snake.

As I continued hitching, I kept looking for the battered Volvo, but I never saw it again. The drivers who now picked me up would talk about the weather or the news. Had I heard about the recent economic crisis in my country? one of them asked me.

"No, I haven't heard about it," I said, scarcely able to conceal my boredom.

Off the Beach

UP AND DOWN, TWISTING and turning like a demented snake, the road wound through a realm of fervent green punctuated by precipitous cliffs. Occasionally, it would take us through a village of low-slung shingle houses that was like a vision from an earlier, not to mention a sleepier, era. Occasionally, too, it boasted bumper-scraping ruts and seemingly bottomless potholes, features you seldom expect on a major road.

At one point my guide, a young man named Ossie, brought our vehicle to an abrupt halt. Some sort of procession was coming our way. Young and old, healthy and infirm, a hundred or so people were dancing and singing as well as rhythmically clapping their hands. Their merry mood was so infectious that I felt like getting out of the car and joining them. Then I saw a donkey pulling a cart with a coffin on top of it.

"Did the local tax collector die?" I asked Ossie.

"This is how all our funerals are," he said. "Jolly until they reach the graveyard, then there'll be crying and screaming like you've never heard before."

I was so intrigued by this spectacle that I didn't think to take a picture of it, or even take a picture of the ancient-looking man bringing up the rear whom Ossie said was the local witch doctor.

You will perhaps be surprised to learn that I was not in some remote part of Africa or South America, but the Caribbean. Yes, the same Caribbean whose islands, the travel industry would have you believe, consist entirely of white sand beaches on which the only footprints are your own.

As it happens, St. Vincent—the island I was visiting—has no white beaches, only black ones whose sand is so hot that I tried to avoid leaving my footprints on them. Except for when I found myself with a canopy of rainforest overhead, I could look up wherever I happened to be on the island and see the source of this sand—a 4,048-foot volcano named La Soufrière. And not only does this volcano create beaches, it also enriches St. Vincent's already rich soil every time it erupts (last eruption: 1979).

Rather than burn my feet on a fiery beach, I decided to put them to use on an often fiery mountain, so I set out to climb La Soufrière with a guide named Irocki.

Up we hiked, through bamboo groves and across orchid-filled ravines. Every once in a while, Irocki would point to a plant—a wild begonia, for instance, or the so-called Part of a Man Life bush—and tell me that it would cure my headache or toothache, help my asthma, lower my blood pressure, or ease the itching of my scabies.

Whatever doubts I might have had about the efficacy of this bush medicine vanished when I tripped on a tree root and landed on a sharp basaltic rock. My left arm was bleeding profusely, but Irocki applied a leaf from a low-climbing vine called a corilla (*Momordica charantia*) to it, and lo! the bleeding stopped in a very short time.

"No charge for the procedure, mon," Irocki observed.

As we approached the summit, the vegetation, first luxuriant, then more scrub-like, gave way to a moonscape of ash and gravel. At last we were standing at the rim of a mile-wide crater. From inside this crater, there was a rising plume of sulphurous smoke shaped like, it seemed to me, an exclamation point.

And squatting a few feet away from us was another exclamation point, albeit of a rather different shape—a large yellowish cane toad with part of a butterfly sticking out of its mouth.

From my elevated position, I gazed out on the Grenadines, the tourist-laden islands extending south from St. Vincent, and I felt a certain pity for all those poor souls who might now be sunning themselves on Bequia or Mustique. Splayed out in the sun, daubing themselves with various lotions, they were missing out on all the fun.

Having climbed up La Soufrière from the windward side, we climbed down on the volcano's leeward side. Not long after we began our descent, I looked across a steeply rising gully and noticed some farmers industriously working their fields. Their crop, at once illegal and St. Vincent's major agricultural product, was ganja (aka marijuana). But for this herb, the island's economy probably would sink into a Third World slough. Doubtless this is one reason why the government's attempts to eradicate the herb in question have been somewhat half-hearted.

Toward the end of the trek, we walked along the bottom of a dry river, the Larikai, whose steep walls were so cavelike that there were bats roosting in them. And so close together were these walls that it was impossible not to brush against some of the bat roosts, with the result that we found ourselves more or less covered with guano.

At the actual end of the trek, there was a beach. Did I lie down on its sand and bask in the sun's rays? No, I walked across the beach and waded into the surf, there to wash the bat guano and volcanic debris from my body. I might add that the only footprints on the beach's black sand were Irocki's and my own.

Marooned

SINCE THE WORDS TRAVEL and travail are etymologically linked, I'm now going to tell you a tale of travel travail.

Some years ago, an old fisherman named Hector dropped me off on Mingulay, a nine-mile-square rock of an island in Scotland's Outer Hebrides. In 1908, Mingulay's inhabitants relocated to the more user-friendly islands of Vatersay and Barra, and nobody has lived there since. Remote in 1908, the island was even more remote when I was deposited there; so remote, in fact, that cartographers occasionally omit it from their maps.

Hector had promised to pick me up at six o'clock that evening, but six o'clock rolled by and there was no sign of him. Nor was there any sign of him at seven, eight, or nine o'clock. I convinced myself that he'd actually told me six o'clock the following morning, and after a relatively sleepless night, I went to the outcropping of gneiss that served as Mingulay's landing place. No Hector. He didn't show up at six that evening, either. My initial annoyance turned to panic when I realized that I was marooned on what appeared to be a desert island...an unusually wet desert island.

I had brought along a few chocolate bars, and I figured I could stretch them only so far, eating a small chunk now, another chunk later, before starvation set in. Starvation! Would the experience be painful, simply unpleasant, or would I just sink into a stupor? I imagined the local jackdaws descending on my remains with enthusiasm, as those remains would provide a welcome change of diet from the carcasses of the island's near-feral sheep.

Something told me not give up just yet. After all, I wasn't particularly hungry—panic does a good job of keeping hunger at bay. But my panic subsided as I began gathering sorrel and wild celery from the island's nettled hillsides. Here was, if not a bounty of wild edibles, at least enough greens to keep me going for a while. I found a rusty skillet in an old midden heap and cooked up some limpets and mussels that I'd harvested from a tide pool. I varied this somewhat basic bouillabaise by adding *Lycoperdon* puffballs or wild rhubarb to it.

By the third day, my stomach wasn't growling, but purring contentedly. I can survive here, I told myself, and with that awareness came a rush of satisfaction. Meanwhile, I stopped thinking of the island as a desolate and forbidding place.

Apart from a church, which had a lock on its door, the only inhabitable structure on Mingulay was a decrepit sheep fank. Inside the fank, there were several dead ewes, one of which seemed to have died while lambing. The odor was so rank that I gagged the first few times I went in. But the alternative to sleeping in the fank was sleeping outside in the cold drizzle that seemed to be the only kind of weather on Mingulay. So I removed the ewes, and although the rank odor remained, I grew more or less accustomed to my quarters.

I still scanned the sea for Hector's boat, although now I felt less alarmed when I didn't see it. Increasingly, the island beckoned to me, and I found myself responding to it. I investigated a crofter's cottage, now hardly more than a heap of rubble, and discovered the remains of an old hand loom. I stood atop a cliff and watched puffins fly off in all directions like tracer bullets. In the southern part of the island, I also discovered what appeared to be an ancient standing stone on top of which sat a jackdaw.

Toward the end of my enforced visit, I came to the realization that there were a lot worse places where I could deposit my bones than Mingulay.

On the morning of the sixth day, Hector's fishing boat arrived with the scent of hot grease coughed up by its antique pistons. A much younger man than Hector stood at the helm, however. He greeted me with a hug, then handed me a beaker of whiskey. "I was almost certain ye'd be dead, laddie," the man—Hector's nephew—exclaimed.

It turned out that Hector had gone back to his home in Castlebay, Barra, after dropping me off, and as he was climbing up the town's steep slipway, he suffered a stroke. He'd been in a coma for almost five days. Upon regaining consciousness, his first stricken words were: "I've left a man on Mingulay..."

"How is Hector doing now?" I asked the nephew.

"Just fine, laddie. Just fine."

As the boat was chugging away from Mingulay, I confess that I felt something akin to regret. For I was surrendering a rare privilege, one all too infrequently experienced by travelers nowadays—the privilege of travail.

An Arctic Munchausen

In the 1930s and 1940s, a man named Jan Welzl lived in the Yukon Territory's Dawson City, a town more or less surrounded by goldfields. Unlike other Dawsonites, however, Welzl did not prospect for gold. Instead, he occupied himself with the construction of a perpetual motion machine. This contraption was composed of various pipe fittings, axles, and counterweights, as well as the occasional beer bottle or tin can; it also had a cavorting ball, to which Welzl—called "John Inventor" by his neighbors—would point and, in his typically broken English, say: "She go up, she go down, she go 'yah, yah, yah.'"

Welzl is remembered in Dawson as a harmless eccentric, a man who hurt no one but himself, since his invention blocked access to his stove and thus prevented him from eating. No doubt his neighbors would have been surprised to learn that the unconventional Czech had recently been at the center of a literary controversy.

The book that inspired this controversy, *Thirty Years in the Golden North*, first appeared in English in 1932. As a selection of the prestigious Book of the Month Club, it sold more than 150,000 copies in only a few months. Macmillan, the publisher, marketed it as nonfiction, but some of its reviewers thought it might be a bit more fancy than fact.

Arctic explorer Vilhjalmur Stefansson, in a letter (entitled "Hakluyt or Hoax") to the *Saturday Review of Literature*, went one step further. He proposed that *Thirty Years in the Golden North* should be considered a parody of exploration literature or, if not a parody, a complete fabrication. For no one had recently lived in the New Siberian Islands, the remote archipelago that Welzl claimed had been his Arctic home and which he populated with numerous "polar settlers" and Eskimo inhabitants.

Stefansson, a rather humorless man, did not bother to catalogue the hundreds of outrageous details posing as facts in the book, so I'll list a few:

1. Welzl's Arctic mailmen typically attach 24 sledges together and harness 350 dogs to these sledges, with the lead dog half a mile ahead of its 349 companions.
2. His Eskimos worship monkey idols twenty-five-feet tall and engage in boxing matches in their kayaks.
3. People who have toothaches in the Golden North purposefully get scurvy, because with scurvy their gums become so spongy that the offending tooth simply falls out.

And then there's the question of Welzl's descriptions of his own Arctic travels. From his purported base in the

New Siberian Islands, he journeys now to San Francisco, now to Nome, and now to the Mackenzie Delta with such casualness that he could be sauntering down the street to the local convenience store. You can imagine him saying that he discovered the North Pole on a weekend getaway.

I'll now let you in on a little secret: Jan Welzl did not write *Thirty Years in the Golden North*. Rather, he dictated it.

In the mid-1920s, Welzl returned to Czechoslovakia from wherever he'd been in the Arctic and, more or less indigent, began giving lectures on his travels. In one of these lectures, he advanced the theory that kangaroos would make better sled animals than dogs; in another, he claimed to have found a race of pygmy Eskimos who'd arrived on a meteor from Mars. He would put salt on his maps of the Arctic to indicate the presence of a glacier, only to have his glacier licked clean by the village dogs.

Lecturing did not bring in much money, so Welzl started sending articles to newspapers. There was one problem with this idea: the man who signed his articles "Bear Eater" or "An Arctic Bismarck" was a terrible writer. But because these articles about his Siberian adventures seemed to contain some good stories, they were passed on to two legitimate writers, a pair of journalists named Bedrich Golombek and Edvard Valenta. The two men decided that their garrulous countryman had a book in him...as long as he didn't write it himself.

Welzl talked, and the journalists took notes. He talked some more, spitting gobs of tobacco in all directions, and they took more notes while trying to dodge the tobacco. A month passed, then two months. Sometimes Welzl would ask for rum, in his words, "to get my memory back." And the journalists would be only too happy to oblige him, because his stories got even better when fueled by drink. In one story, an Eskimo shaman provides a Laplander named Pitt with a new nose (the old nose had been frostbitten, and Pitt lost it when he sneezed). Golombek and Valenta must have been particularly generous with their allotments of rum while Welzl was telling them this yarn.

And so *Thirty Years in the Golden North* (Czech title: *Tricet Let Na Zlatem Severu*) was born. A year later, in 1933, another book entitled *The Quest for Polar Treasure* came out. Although this second book has some notably Welzlian tidbits—for example, thirty-six-foot-tall Arctic octopi with deformed human faces that like nothing better than to crush unwary explorers to death—you can't help but feel that it consists primarily of leavings Golombek and Valenta scraped from the bottom of Welzl's barrel.

Meanwhile, Welzl himself had traveled north again. He wanted to go back to Siberia, but because of ice on the Yukon River and also because he'd run out of money, he got only as far as Dawson City. Dawson, which in many ways was as eccentric as he was, appealed to Welzl, so he decided to settle there.

The availability of junk appealed to him as well. At places like the Yukon Sheet Metal Works, he began collecting scrap materials for his new obsession: a perpetual motion machine. By trying to build something that would always be on the move, he may have been compensating for the fact that his own travels were now virtually at an end.

In 1934, Welzl learned that *Thirty Years in the Golden North* had become a best seller. You can imagine his consternation. On the one hand, he had signed away his rights to the book, so he couldn't cash in on its success. On the other hand, the book contained a certain amount of material that he didn't recognize as his own. So he took a middle road, simultaneously denying that the book was his and demanding royalties for it. Welzl even denied that he'd had an actual contract. He said Golombek had pointed a loaded revolver at him and announced that this revolver was his contract.

In a letter to Stefansson, Welzl claimed to be a pauper. But his habits were so frugal that he hardly needed much money. All he seemed to need were parts for his perpetual motion machine, and these he could gather free of charge in his walks around town. He was a familiar figure in Dawson, an inveterate collector of whatever no one else wanted, from discarded tires to rusty tin cans. Almost everything he found became part of his invention, which, by the end of his life, had grown so large that it stuck out the windows of his cabin.

On September 18, 1948 Jan Welzl died at the age of eighty. He died, I should say, after a fashion, for he was reborn in Communist Czechoslovakia a few years later.

In his new incarnation, "Eskimo Welzl" (as he was affectionately called) became a symbol of unfettered individualism. He had lived the life of his choice, without any rules imposed on him by officialdom. True, it was a rather eccentric life, but at least it was his life. And in passages like the following, from *Thirty Years in the Golden North*, he seems to be attacking Communism well before his country became Communist: "There is true liberty up North. Nobody is limited in his freedom... Whatever you see, you can go after...there is nothing to stop you." A Prague astronomer later named an asteroid (#15425) after this doughty celebrant of freedom.

In the early 1950s, Czechs began making pilgrimages to Welzl's grave in the Catholic Cemetery in Dawson. When I visited the grave myself in 1992, someone had placed a boot on it, a tribute to Welzl's erstwhile wandering habit, and the cross was so laden with wreaths that it seemed in danger of toppling over.

Truth to tell, this cross did not mark Welzl's grave. It seems that an early Czech visitor had simply gone to the cemetery, picked out a convenient cross, and tacked Welzl's name onto it. In all probability, Welzl's admirers were laying their wreaths on the grave of an itinerant Italian laborer named Peter Fagetti. Welzl's own final resting place is unknown, a fate somehow appropriate for a man who seemed not to have a single conventional bone in his body.

A Woman in the Polar Night

I'VE NEVER BEEN ATTRACTED to the luminaries of Arctic exploration. Sir John Franklin, Commodore Robert Peary, Frederick Cook, and Adolphus Greely—they've always struck me as an unpleasantly obsessive bunch, and with the exception of Cook, who was a convicted felon, a rather humorless bunch as well. At least one of them, Peary, had the disposition of a predaceous corporate tycoon. "Mine at last!" he exclaimed upon attaining (or not attaining) the Pole, as if he'd just engineered a hostile takeover.

Christiane Ritter was neither an explorer or a luminary. Instead, she was a well-to-do Austrian *hausfrau* who, prior to her year in Svalbard, had never strayed from her comfortable surroundings. Yet perhaps because she had no interest in an Arctic Grail, whether the Pole, the Northwest Passage, or just an Unknown Land, she could appreciate the Arctic in ways that the aforementioned luminaries, wrapped in their grail-oriented blinders, could not. And in appreciating the Arctic, indeed thriving in it, she gave the lie to the notion that women do not belong at the ends of the earth.

A less likely person to visit the Arctic, much less develop a passion for it, would be hard to imagine. The thirty-six-year-old Christiane had agreed to join her husband Hermann in Svalbard after reading his diaries, which (she observed) hardly included any mention "of cold or darkness, storms or hardship." She decided that this would be a good place to knit socks and read long novels. Her friends and, later, the passengers on the cruise ship that brought her to Svalbard were appalled: a woman's place was, if not in the home, at least not in a geography so lacking in the usual amenities.

Svalbard was close enough to Europe that its wildlife had been plundered for over three hundred years prior to Christiane's arrival in 1934. Still, its primal quality had remained an inspiration to numerous Europeans, including Hermann Ritter, who had made repeated trips to Svalbard, first in 1913, as a youthful deckhand on the Prince of Monaco's yacht, and later as a hunter-trapper. In fact, it's hard to say which was greater, his love for Svalbard or his love for his wife. Those two loves combined in his desire to have Christiane join him in a place called Grahuken (Gray Hook), so named because of the grey Devonian rocks in the area.

The utter wretchedness of their hut ("a small, bleak, bare box") disturbed Christiane, at least at first. She was even more disturbed that another person, a Norwegian trapper named Karl Nicholaisen, would be sharing the cramped hut with her and her husband. For his part, Karl expected Christiane to go crazy sooner or later, probably sooner, and he figured that the manifestations of this craziness would provide him with (as he later told explorer Willie Knutsen) "some mid-winter entertainment." Later he changed his opinion of her, telling Knutsen that she was "one hell of a woman."

Stuck in the hut by herself during an epic snowstorm, Christiane almost did go crazy. At the same time she realized that, however tough the circumstances, she could survive them. And from then on, she did not think of the Arctic as an enemy. Rather, it was a realm "where everything goes its prescribed way...without human intervention." Such was her transformation that she could even suggest that "in centuries to come, people will go to the Arctic as in biblical times they withdrew to the desert, to find the truth again." I can't imagine any Arctic explorer making a statement like that.

Christiane wrote an extraordinary book, *A Woman in the Polar Night*, about her transformation. Before she wrote it, she had written nothing of consequence. As "mad Ireland" (in W. H. Auden's phrase) hurt Yeats into poetry, frigid Svalbard seems to have had the same effect on her, although it did not hurt so much as invigorate her. At one point, she describes a landscape of "frozen splendor" whose clarity makes it seem at once palpable and remote, worthy, certainly, of a photograph. She starts to reach for her camera, then pauses and makes this observation: "It seems to me a deadly sin to steal a piece of this supernatural scene and carry it away with me." She doesn't take the photograph.

A personal aside: I wish that contemporary camera-wielders could read this passage in Christiane's book. Do these folks actually see what they're photographing? Get rid of that bloody camera, I've often wanted to tell them, and use those twin orbs in your head commonly called eyes, lest they become vestigial.

Christiane left what she called "the Arctic wilderness" in June of 1935, never to return. Hermann himself did return to the Arctic several years later when the Wehrmacht forced him to command a German weather station in northeast Greenland during World War II. Northeast Greenland resembles Svalbard in many respects, but Captain Ritter, who was neither a Nazi or a supporter of the Nazi cause, could not have been more miserable. Ironically, one of his mandates was to capture a Dane named Henry Rudi, a trapper he'd known in Svalbard. Even more ironically, the Norwegian government banned Hermann from Svalbard for the rest of his life because he'd been a German officer, albeit an unwilling one, during the War.

As for Christiane, she didn't really need to return to the Arctic wilderness, since she brought it back with her, or at least brought back a radically different way of looking at the world. Not long after she got back to Austria, her house burned to the ground, but rather than mourn its loss and the loss of all her possessions, she was grateful.

For she could now live simply, without a surfeit of ballast, just as she'd lived in Grahuken.

"A year in the Arctic should be compulsory to everyone," she would say to friends and family, indeed everyone she knew, adding: "Then you will come to realize what's important in this life...and what isn't."

An Unfair Trade

In 1667, THE DUTCH made one of the most lopsided real estate deals in history: they traded an obscure New World island called Manhattan to the English for Rhun, a tiny island in the East Indies. Rhun abounded in nutmeg, the gold of the spice trade, whereas Manhattan's nutmeg was nonexistent. The Dutch must have felt that they'd pulled a fast one on their long-time rivals.

Today Manhattan can boast a giant pulsing city, but what about Rhun? Finding myself on nearby Banda Neira, the main island in Indonesia's Banda Archipeligo, I decided to visit a place every bit as obscure now (it doesn't even appear in the recent *The Times Atlas of the World*) as Manhattan was in 1667.

A pair of Australian divers and I chartered a fishing boat, and off we chugged into the Banda Sea. The three-hour trip passed without incident until one of the Australians started trolling, and a sea eagle swooped down and snatched his lure. Suddenly he had an eagle at the end of his hook. Note: Eagles tend to be considerably harder to disengage from a hook than a fish.

At last we began to smell a heady, languorous fragrance—the scent of nutmeg. Then we were approaching an archetypal tropical island fringed with palm trees. Rhun has a dangerous sunken reef, so we anchored well offshore and paddled our dinghy toward the nearest beach.

The moment we landed, the previously deserted beach was swarming with a boisterous group of people eager to see the exotic Westerners. One man grabbed my hand and shook it so vigorously that I wondered if he wanted to break it off and take it home as a souvenir of our visit.

The crowd followed us through the village to the house of the *orang besar* (headman), piling in until the room came to resemble the famous stateroom scene in the Marx Brothers' film *A Night at the Opera*.

The *orang besar* was a cordial, elaborately tatooed man who seemed to be trying very hard to keep his cool at the sight of oddities like us. As we drank cups of tea, we engaged him in a brief Q&A session. I asked when was the last time Westerners showed up here.

"Maybe two years ago, maybe three," he said.

"And how many people live on Rhun?" one of the Australians asked.

"Forty-nine grandfathers," the *orang besar* answered proudly.

Apparently, non-grandfathers were non-persons, at least as far as the local census was concerned. And why not? Unlike a child or even a sub-adult, an elder can offer wisdom based on a long lifetime of experience.

Now it was the *orang besar*'s turn to pose a few questions, and he asked us why we were visiting his flyspeck of an island. The Australians told me that, being divers, they wanted to look for old shipwrecks on the reef. When I told him that I was a writer, his eyes lit up. "Maybe you will bring tourists to Rhun?" he said.

I winced...inwardly, of course. The last thing this island needed was tourists, who, intentionally or not, incite a mercantile urge wherever they go. I would hate to come back here some day and see heaps of "I LOVE RHUN" T-shirts or postcards juxtaposing Manhattan's skyscrapers with Rhun's conspicuous absence of them. "To get tourists, you need attractions," I told the *orang besar*.

Now we can change the subject, I thought. I was mistaken. The *orang besar* suggested that I visit an old fort called El Dorado built by the Spanish but subsequently taken over by the English. He drew me a map of how to get to this attraction.

I walked back through the village with a parade of barefoot kids running ahead of, alongside, and behind me. A bit slower, but also barefoot, was one of Rhun's forty-nine grandfathers: he was in a *sopi* (palm wine) haze, and he tried to kiss my hand, a gesture that probably harkened back to Dutch colonial times.

"Where you from, mister?" one of the kids asked me.

Along with other Indonesians, the folks on Rhun call all Westerners, including women, "mister." This also seemed to be a survival from colonial times, when residents of the East Indies were obliged to call a Dutchman "Mynheer."

"I'm from America," I said.

"Is it a big or a little island?"

"It's a big, big island..."

Now I paused to rest from the heat. I sat down and opened my copy of Somerset Maugham's *The Narrow Corner*, a novel set in and around a fictionalized Banda Neira. My escorts paused to rest, too. They stared at my book as if it were the world's greatest curiosity. When I turned it upside down, they continued to stare at it, but also stared back at me. Ah, he reads upside down, they may have been telling themselves—an insight into the baffling ways of Westerners.

And then I was following a path through a grove of willowy nutmeg trees. I saw polka-dotted butterflies with six-inch wingspans, brilliant orange spiders, and a marsupial cuscus asleep in one of the nutmeg trees. I also heard the "Aw-aw-aw" of the nutmeg pigeon, a handsome green-collared bird that gives the lie to the notion that pigeons are simply rats with wings.

At last I reached El Dorado, which turned out to be hardly more than a heap of crumbling stones. If I hadn't been told that these stones had once been part of a fort, I would have assumed that they were volcanic debris, an item quite common in these parts.

I wasn't disappointed, however. For an immaculately preserved fort would have seemed presumptuous on this unassuming little island. Indeed, anything from beyond the reef would have seemed presumptuous here. For Rhun was a place wholly itself, wholly idiosyncratic, and I wouldn't have exchanged it for all the Manhattans in the world.

Into Cold Water

I ONCE TAUGHT ENGLISH in Iceland, and whenever I had any free time, I would hang out with the pilots at the Reykjavik airport. I recommend this sort of social interaction to every adventurous traveler, for pilots can take you to places that are either off the map or clutching that map's obscure edges.

One day I was drinking cup after cup of coffee (no self-respecting Icelander ever stops with one or even two cups of coffee) with a pilot named Helgi, who, I learned, had an Inuit girlfriend in Kap Dan, Greenland, and several times a month flew his Mitsubishi turboprop across Denmark Strait to visit her.

"Maybe you need a navigator for your trips?" I asked Helgi. Needless to say, I had no idea how to read aeronautical charts.

"Nej," he told me, "but you can come along to keep me company."

So I began going to a part of Greenland unvisited by outsiders until as recently as 1884, when Captain Gustav Holm of the Royal Danish Navy traveled up Greenland's east coast in search of the lost Norse colonies. Captain Holm found an uncontacted people, the Tunumiut, who assumed he and his fellow Danes were the offspring of a Tunumiut woman who'd once mated with her dog. How else explain their curious behavior and equally curious skin color, not to mention their totally incomprehensible language?

On one of my trips with Helgi, I borrowed a state-of-the-art camera from an Icelandic friend and put it to energetic use. I took pictures of dogsleds parked like cars in front of every house or tent; I took pictures of the dogs themselves, wild-looking animals with wolfish glints in their eyes; and I took pictures of Tunumiut elders whose wrinkled faces resembled contours on a topo map.

At one point, I was backing up to get a panoramic photo of Kap Dan itself. I lost my footing and tumbled down a steep slope and through the ice (this was already late November) of Angmagssalik Fjord. The cold—the harshest, most brutal cold I've ever experienced—struck me like a flying brick. The water was probably not any colder than thirty-two degrees Fahrenheit, but water sucks the heat out of you twenty-five times faster than air at the same temperature.

How long I was flailing about in the water I don't know, maybe two or three hypothermic minutes. I also spent a hypothermic minute or two trying unsuccessfully to locate my friend's camera at the bottom of the fjord.

I don't remember clawing my way up the steep slope, either. But if I hadn't somehow managed to get up that slope, I doubt that I'd be around to write these words.

Several locals saw what must have looked like an ice-clad apparition swaying with stiff-legged steps in their direction. At first they just stared, but when they realized that I was a human being rather than one of the monsters with which their culture is so generously populated, they quickly covered me with a blanket and helped me to the village infirmary.

The resident nurse, a young Tunumiut woman trained in Denmark, made me remove my clothes, which—because I was shivering so much—I did with some difficulty. After she put warm compresses on my skin, she gave me a cup of hot tea, but my grip was so unsteady that almost none of the tea made it to my mouth. I also chipped a tooth as a result of shivering so violently.

Meanwhile, Helgi had appeared, and he gave me a vigorous Icelandic massage. This only made me feel like I'd been run over by a tank, and I continued to shiver.

By now, half of the village had crowded into the infirmary. Little children, elders, burly seal hunters, teenage girls with babies in their *amautis*—they were all gazing at this mostly naked white man who seemed to have the shakes and who also had one of his eyes frozen shut. Not a few of them found that white man a source of considerable amusement.

Then an elderly woman approached me. Her hair was dressed in a topknot, her eyes were narrow slits pressed deep into her forehead, and she walked like a duck full of eggs. She looked exactly like the sort of person the village would call upon to stop somebody's spasmodic shivering, a state that was doubtless the consequence of a run-in with a *tupilak* (evil spirit).

The old woman began rubbing a sticky substance into my skin. Probably seal grease, I thought. Or maybe walrus, whale, or polar bear grease. Yet the substance in question seemed vaguely familiar, and I asked the nurse what it was.

"We call it Crisco," she said.

Apparently, the application of Crisco was a common practice here. Fall out of your kayak, and you'll have Crisco slathered onto you. Get marooned on an ice floe, and if you survive, you'll end up covered with Crisco. The nurse testified to its efficacy; it sealed up the pores like a package, she told me, and thus kept precious heat bottled up inside you.

As the old woman was basting virtually every inch of my palpitating body, I felt my core temperature begin to rise. This was a strongly physical sensation, as if something inside me was actively engaged in banishing the cold from my body. I could now move my limbs without feeling they would break off into icy chunks. I could also drink the hot tea that the nurse gave me without spilling it. Half an hour later, I stopped shivering altogether.

The traditional remedy of Crisco had triumphed.

Many years have passed since this incident. Yet I still recall my plunge into the icy waters of East Greenland whenever I eat a cookie that's moist and chewy or a cake that's high and light.

The Lizard of Oz

NOT TOO LONG AGO, I picked up an old travel book about Puerto Rico and read of a rare giant lizard, *Anolis rooseveltii*, on the island of Culebra. "Fame will visit anyone who finds this elusive creature," the author of the book proclaimed. Since Fame had thus far given me a wide berth, I hopped a plane to San Juan, then a smaller plane to Culebra.

By the time I arrived on the island, the lizard had shrunk. The book had described it as four feet long, but the local Fish & Wildlife person told me that it was no more than a foot long from snout to vent—hardly competition for a *T. rex*. Still, *A. rooseveltii* is a *T. rex* compared to other anoles, which are among the smallest of all lizards. I also learned that this giant among anoles hadn't been sighted since 1932. Not officially sighted, that is. But there were anecdotal reports of it being seen in the forested areas on Monte Resaca, Culebra's highest summit (height: 650 feet), as recently as a few years ago.

Thus I drove to Monte Resaca and began bushwhacking. Trusting to serendipity, I expected to see the anole in question basking on every boulder or ascending every gumbo-limbo tree. I was so intent in my search that I lost all sense of direction and ended up in someone's backyard.

A Culebran tending his garden looked up at me in surprise. My usual ploy when I trespass like this is to advance confidently toward the person, shake his hand, and announce with a punctilious English accent: "Dr. Basil Withers of the British Antarctic Survey. Jolly good to meet you, old chap."

Since this ploy would not work in the subtropics, I said, "Hello, señor. Seen any big *lagartos* around here lately?"

"*Sí,*" the man replied. "All the time."

"Where's their habitat?" I asked him excitedly.

"My bathroom..." He invited me to inspect his bathroom, where I saw the *lagartos* skittering around on the wall. But they were geckoes, not anoles, and they weren't even all that big.

Serendipity had gotten me nowhere, so I contacted an expat, Beverly Macintyre, who knew the island's backcountry intimately. She mentioned a particular boulder canyon on Monte Resaca, just the sort of place, she said, where a giant anole might hang out. Then she referred to recent development on Culebra: if it continued at its current breakneck pace, then a lot more creatures than *A. rooseveltii* would be in trouble.

In our search for the lizard, Beverly and I entered not so much the forest primeval as the forest prickly. Ground-hugging cacti jabbed us; mesquite bushes stabbed us;

saw-toothed bromeliads slashed at us; and a plant known locally as Fire Man (*Tragia volubilis*) delivered stings that make the stings of a stinging nettle seem positively genteel.

We did not see a giant anole. We did not even see one of the small anoles that reputedly are common on the island. But we did see a discarded McDonald's hamburger wrapper. Note: There is no McDonald's on Culebra.

The next day I decided to take a respite from my search, whereupon I began noticing other curious sights on the island. A sign in a shop window in Dewey, Culebra's only town, said: "Open Some Days, Closed Others." There was also a road sign that said *Termina Carretera* (End of the Road) when in fact the road did not end at all. I wondered if the sign was a reference to the cemetery only a hundred or so yards away and thus not a road sign at all.

In the evening, I visited a pleasantly sleazy bar in Dewey and discovered that a number of its patrons had been kidnapped by extraterrestrials. "Hasn't everybody, señor?" one man told me. "They [the extraterrestrials] feed you really well," another man said. Talking to them, I began to think that I had fetched up on some sort of Caribbean fantasy island—an ideal habitat for, among other things, an incredibly shrinking lizard.

Several days later, I still hadn't found any evidence of an *A. rooseveltii* on the island. My trip was coming to an end, so I asked Teresa Tallevast, the manager of the Culebra Wildlife Refuge, if there were any area that I might have overlooked. She suggested that I check out the trail that wound down from Monte Resaca to Playa Resaca.

So I began hiking on this steepdown trail. Occasionally, I would stop and peer into the surrounding bush. Once I did see a finned reptilian tail disappear into a tangle of mesquite, but that could have been my imagination...or an iguana. Once I reached the bottom, the trail began meandering through a labyrinth of white mangroves; I looked up at their gnarled branches and then down at their arching prop roots. Still no anole.

At last I came out on Playa Resaca, a long empty swathe of yellow sand. The sun was blisteringly hot, but I didn't go for a swim. *Resaca* means undertow in Spanish (it's also a metaphor for a hangover), and if I had gone swimming, I might have washed ashore on the west coast of Africa or, at the very least, on one of the Virgin Islands.

All of a sudden I saw what appeared to be the tread marks of large truck in the sand. I was outraged. But then I realized that those tread marks were actually the flipper imprints of a female leatherback turtle who'd come ashore the night before to lay her eggs. Weighing a thousand pounds or more, leatherbacks are an endangered species. I counted myself extremely lucky even to see the tracks of one.

And so it was that my quest for a rare reptile on Culebra ended in success.

The Worst Place
in the World

WikiTravel notwithstanding, Clipperton does not have any hotels, restaurants, or nightlife. Indeed, the island—an extraordinarily hot, waterless, more or less uninhabitable landfall 700 miles southwest of Tejupan Point, Mexico—mostly consists of shit. More specifically, it consists of the guano of two seabird species, masked and brown boobies, both of which nest on Clipperton in the thousands.

Once upon a time you would not wrinkle your nose at a thought of a place like Clipperton. You might even try to acquire rights to it, as the U.S., France, England, and Mexico did in the 19th and 20th centuries. The U.S. even passed legislation in 1856 that proclaimed any guano-rich island not owned by another country American property. For the extremely high nitrogen content of guano made it at least as valuable as gold.

In 1909, Mexico settled a garrison on Clipperton in an attempt to resolve the issue of the island's ownership. The post was manned by a Captain Ramon da Arnaud, twelve soldiers, and a huge Carib Indian named Victoriano, who worked the newly built lighthouse. Wives and children swelled the population to thirty, a quite-large number for a place incapable of producing its own food.

On June 16, 1914, the last supply ship from the mainland visited the island. Whereupon Mexico, which was in the middle of a Civil War, either forgot about Clipperton or put it at the bottom of its list of priorities. What resulted from this oversight is a survival story that makes most other desert island survival stories seem like cotton candy.

Clipperton remains a not very pleasant place even if, like me, you have the benefit of a fully equipped scientific research vessel moored offshore. I could tolerate the ubiquitous land crabs and the rats, both of which seemed to regard me as a food product. I could even tolerate the overwhelming smell of boobie guano, which permeated my clothes. But I couldn't tolerate the heat. One day when the temperature reached 112°F, I thought: if Hell is anything like this, I am going to mend my ways.

But back to our marooned garrison. In the first few months, Captain da Arnaud rationed the island's few coconuts so that each person received one per week. The rest of the post's diet consisted of the salt-ridden flesh of boobies. The brackish lagoon kept away fish, but not sharks. To the castaways, the endless circling of dorsal fins must have seemed a bit ominous.

Soon Clipperton's inhabitants began to die, some of starvation, others of scurvy. A ship was sighted on the horizon; the ship was probably a mirage, but Captain da

Arnaud and his men began rowing toward it. Their decrepit dingy capsized almost immediately on the reef, and the Captain and his men drowned within shouting range of their wives. A few days later, an arm and part of a leg washed ashore, presumably the only parts of the men the sharks hadn't eaten.

Worse was yet to come. Shortly after Captain da Arnaud's death, a hurricane destroyed all the buildings on the island. The sun was now even more murderous than before. Daily exposure to its rays drove the lighthouse keeper Victoriano mad, and he killed the last two soldiers, then declared himself King of Clipperton. His first royal decree was to make the remaining women his concubines. Any woman who resisted his advances he would fling to the sharks.

While I was on Clipperton, I sometimes thought I heard eerie female sobs, especially at night. But I never seemed able to locate the source of these sobs. My expedition mates figured I was hearing the wind soughing in the palm trees or perhaps the cooing of boobies. Myself, I'm not so sure...

The lighthouse keeper had his way with nearly all of the surviving women. On July 18, he approached Señora da Arnaud, the Captain's widow and one of the few women who continued to resist him. As he tried to grab her, she planted an axe firmly in his skull. A few days later, the U.S. Navy gunship *Yorktown*, which had been scouring the Pacific for German naval bases, appeared on the horizon. More than three years had passed since the last Mexican supply ship had raised its anchor. When Captain Perrill and several of his men went ashore, they found a colony of eleven emaciated women and children, several of whom did not even have the energy to slip on clothing at the arrival of their visitors.

Captain Perrill removed this last bedraggled remnant of the garrison to Salina Cruz on the Mexican mainland. Neither Perrill, his men, nor Señora da Arnaud told the authorities about what happened to the lighthouse keeper, so those authorities doubtless assumed that Victoriano had died of scurvy or starvation like most of the island's inhabitants.

The rest of Clipperton's story is anti-climactic. In 1931, an arbiter rendered a decision on the island's ownership: it became the property of France, not Mexico. But France did not exploit Clipperton, because guano was no longer a viable commodity. Thus the French were now stuck with a place so worthless that even its most valuable asset was worthless.

On my last day on Clipperton, I decided to look for a skull with an axe imbedded in it. I didn't find that skull, but I did end up with heat blisters over the exposed portions of my body. So I carried away a wholly appropriate souvenir from this parched outpost in the Pacific. But not the most appropriate souvenir: that would have been, of course, shit.

Farthest North

NEAR THE OUTSKIRTS of Longyearbyen (pop. 1,500), the main town in Norway's Svalbard archipelago and the world's northernmost community, I noticed an attractive young woman pushing a pram. Nothing particularly unusual about that, except that the woman had a 30.06 rifle slung over her shoulder.

The firearm's message wasn't "Mess with me or my kid, and I'll blow you to Kingdom Come," as it might have been in certain parts of America. Rather, she was carrying it for protection against polar bears. For unlike the gentle-spirited bears in Phillip Pullman's *The Golden Compass*, Svalbard's nonfictional bears sometimes seek out human beings as a dietary supplement to seals. So it's a really good idea to carry a firearm if you're venturing outside of town.

On the other hand, local laws favor wildlife (a reaction against four centuries of promiscuous hunting and trapping), which means that if you shoot a polar bear even in self-defense, you'll be subjected to a legal process hardly less involved than if you killed a fellow human being.

I could imagine myself standing before a Norwegian judge. "Self-defense?" he would exclaim. "Why, you shot that bear in cold blood!"

"It was going to eviscerate me with a single swipe of its paw," I would say. "Ah, but it didn't eviscerate you," the judge would respond gleefully, then pronounce my sentence.

Given this scenario, and given its alternative (being eaten), I decided to hang around Longyearbyen.

Named for John M. Longyear, an early twentieth-century American coal-mining magnate who wanted to turn Svalbard into the West Virginia of the Arctic, the town was not your typical 78° north community. It had a large Thai population as well as the northernmost Thai massage parlor in the world. It had reindeer grazing next to its post office and barnacle geese nesting in its cemetery. Much to my delight, it had a watering hole that boasted the largest selection of single malt Scotch I'd ever seen.

Longyearbyen also had tower trestles, carts, and pieces of metallic debris from its coal-mining past. None of this could be removed, much less sold to a scrap merchant, because all pre-1945 objects are considered part of Svalbard's cultural heritage and protected by law. Such "artifacts" made certain parts of the town seem like a postmodern sculpture park, one whose dominant color was reddish brown—the color of rust.

Another oddity: hardly any of the locals were local. An Iranian named Kazem had converted an old military van into perhaps the world's most northerly kabob wagon; the Thais seemed to do most of the manual labor; and an Alaskan, Mark Sabbatini, edited *Ice People*, which described itself as "the world's northernmost alternative newspaper."

I'd been in Longyearbyen for nearly a week when I got the urge to see what lay beyond the scree slopes surrounding the town. Over a whale-and-mushroom pizza at a local eatery, I planned a hike with a Norwegian friend, who, it goes without saying, owned a firearm.

The following day Sven-Erik and I began climbing a nearby mountain called Plataberget. As we climbed, I could see the aerial tramways of the town's abandoned coal mines in the distance. I could also see the giant golf balls of the satellite station SvalSat; Norwegian leftists did not appreciate the fact that the U.S. used data from Sval-Sat to track sandstorms during the Iraq War.

The mountain's flat summit had pockets of snow, stunted plants, and an abundance of lichen-decorated rocks. Certainly, it didn't have enough snow for a snowmobile—an extremely popular item in Svalbard. So why did I seem to be hearing one?

As it happened, I was hearing Sven-Erik's cellphone—he'd programmed its ringtone to sound like the roar of a snowmobile. "Yes," he told his wife, "I did bring my rifle."

Needless to say, polar bears were seldom far from my mind. "Why do people in Longyearbyen always keep their doors unlocked?" I asked Sven-Erik. "Perhaps so they can make a quick escape from a bear?"

"We keep our doors unlocked because it's very hard to get a key into a frozen lock," he said.

On we hiked. I pointed to what seemed like an ancient archaeological site, only to have my companion tell me that it was the site of a barbecue party from a few years ago.

A short while later, we came to a stone cairn, the so-called *Ninavarden* (Nina Memorial). At this spot, in 1995, a young Norwegian woman named Nina Olaussen was killed by a mountain-climbing bear. She had loved wildlife and assumed that wildlife would love her. One type of wildlife did in fact love her...to death.

"Did she carry a firearm?" I asked Sven-Erik.

"No," he said.

Our own trip was less eventful. We climbed, then glissaded down a crevasse, hiked along a valley, and then wandered into Huset, an upscale bar and restaurant. It looked no different from any other establishment of its kind, except for the gun rack in the vestibule.

Sven-Erik and I toasted each other with glasses of Gilde, a Norwegian aquavit. Then he went home, and I decided to do a little more exploring. I was walking toward the burial ground of the northernmost victims of the 1918 flu epidemic when a large white form emerged from a culvert.

My heart skipped several beats. I tried to be positive about what I figured would happen next. There were billions of human beings on the planet, but only 25,000 or so polar bears. If this one devoured my all-too-common flesh, the imbalance between the two species would be slightly less dramatic. Likewise, the rending of that flesh would be an act of revenge for the climate change vicissitudes to which my species has subjected its species.

But the white form turned out to be only one of Svalbard's reindeer still in its winter coat. Unperturbed by my presence, it trotted off in a leisurely manner. Later I saw it grazing beside one of John M. Longyear's tower trestles, its white coat positively radiant in the non-setting sun.

A Feast on Fais

So UNUSUAL ARE VISITORS to Fais, an outlier of Yap and one of Micronesia's most remote outposts, that I felt all eyes gazing at me as I wandered about the island. "Look," those eyes seemed to say, "he walks upright just like us. He must be a human being, too."

To my own eyes, Fais seemed like a happy combination of the old Pacific and *Monty Python's Flying Circus*. No one was wearing western clothes, not even the torn, permanently smudged T-shirts other Pacific islanders seem to consider the height of fashion. The only book I saw on the island, a Bible, was being used as cigarette paper.

Not surprisingly, Fais had all sorts of taboos, and as much as I tried to act in accordance with them, I kept making gaffes. For example, I needed some sort of shelter on an excruciatingly hot day, so I walked into an official-looking structure with low windows and a thatched roof. I walked back out again right away, for the chorus of nervous female giggles told me that I'd just invaded one of the island's menstrual huts.

If I had been a local, I would have been fined a year's taro crop for this not-inconsiderable blunder. But I was an outsider, and as one of the island's chiefs told me, "American menstrual huts probably look very different from ours."

In spite of my gaffes, the island decided to hold a feast for me the evening before I was scheduled to leave. At first I protested, saying that I was hardly worthy of such attention.

"But we always give *wassolas* (outsiders) like you a feast," another chief explained. I got the impression that even if I had been a visiting child molester, I still would have been given a grand send-off.

If you're sponsoring a feast in this part of Micronesia, you don't just sit down and open a hundred cans of Spam, although Spam is considered haute cuisine throughout the Western Pacific. Nor do you slaughter a pig, a goat, or a monitor lizard. Instead, you go out and kill the appropriate number of fruit bats, a.k.a. flying foxes. These bats are so popular as a feast food in Micronesia that whole colonies of them have been wiped out, and some species are now close to extinction.

So there we were, my hosts and I, seated on mats in the open-sided village meeting house. Except for a few small children, everyone was chewing betel nut. Sitting on a mat confirms a mental state already predisposed toward relaxation, while chewing betel nut—not a real nut, but the seed of the areca palm—produces a mild euphoria, along with a mouth condition that resembles terminal gingivitis.

At last a couple of boys arrived with our recently dispatched entree. Then the *fanihis*, as they're called in Micronesia, were placed in an underground oven and cooked, fur and all. The process took an eternity, since on Fais something isn't cooked until it's overcooked.

I confess that the longer the bats were cooked, the more relieved I felt. For the fruit bat is the primary host of the notorious Nipah virus, and if a bat isn't cooked long enough, it can pass this virus on to the diner. Which could mean, for that diner, a choice array of maladies, including disorientation, encephalitis, convulsions, coma, and—in roughly half the cases—death.

While the bats were cooking, the island's high chief sat down beside me. Through his son, who spoke some English, he asked me how I liked Fais.

Certain idioms get lost in translation, so when I replied that I liked it very much, although it had been hard for a *wassola* like me to get used to so many topless women, the chief looked quite appalled.

"But all our women have heads," he declared.

When I gestured at a couple of women who were naked from the waist up, he seemed not so much appalled as confused. He must have wondered how I could have found my way around the island, given my inability to see an object so obvious as a human head.

Mercifully, the removal of the bats from the oven put an end to our surreal interaction. There was now an expectant hush among my fellow feasters. Soon I had one of the bats in my hand, and then I was making an incision in its furry breast.

The meat didn't have the sweet flavor that I would have expected from a creature whose diet is exclusively fruit. It tasted more like what I would have expected from a creature whose diet is exclusively formaldehyde.

I ate the breast, then pushed aside the rest of the bat, mumbling something about how I preferred the meat even to that of monitor lizard.

But you've hardly begun to eat it, my hosts protested. They pointed to the bat's hairy glandular pouches and large pharyngeal sacs, then made smacking noises with their lips. They pointed to the bat's wings and elongated external ears and made even louder smacking noises. Even the dorsal and pectoral flight muscles inspired them to smack their lips.

Well, at least nothing goes to waste around here, I told myself, and began nibbling on various parts of bat anatomy.

The ears weren't bad. Not bad at all. No, they were downright awful. They tasted like they'd never been irrigated or cleaned. As for the wings, they had the texture and maybe even the flavor of monofilament.

Just when I thought my culinary trials were over, the wizened elder seated next to me pointed to my bat's penis, and with a universal gesture, he indicated that it would put lead in my pencil. Yet another gesture indicated that I should eat it. Now I've dined on plenty of exotic foods—smoked kitten in Borneo, seal eye in Nunavik, big-ass ant (*Hormigas culonas*) in Ecuador, *aivi-kannuunajuuit* (the half-digested stomach contents of a walrus) in East Greenland, and lutefisk in Minnesota—but never bat dick. I can't say the prospect of eating it now appealed to me.

The elder repeated the universal gesture, this time flashing me a lascivious grin. Even though I didn't feel I needed any more lead in my pencil, I figured that I'd be offending my hosts if I refused to eat the bat's penis. Also, every traveler's mantra is (or should be): Eat what your hosts eat, and then you'll understand them a lot better.

So with a quick flick of my knife, I sliced off the bat's organ of generation, popped it in my mouth, chewed and then swallowed what tasted like a piece of leather soaked in Angostura bitters. No, I'm being overly kind: the organ in question tasted like a concentrate of uric acid wrapped in old tire tread.

The feast went on, but the bat's piece de resistance, so to speak, did not make me feel any more lusty than I would have felt if I had eaten a bowl of vanilla yogurt. After it was over, I was heading back to my tent, when a teenage boy with a buzz cut approached me. "That was gross," he said.

"What was gross?" I asked him.

"Eating your *fanihi's* penis," he said. His face was contorted into a grimace.

"But I thought it was the custom around here."

"Maybe long ago, but not anymore. Well, a few old guys might still do it, but they'd get better results if they just watched porn videos..."

Only connect, said English novelist E. M. Forster. And at least I'd connected with one person, the wizened elder...unless, of course, that elder had been pulling my leg. Might he have made a bet with his friends that he could convince the gullible American to eat a *fanihi's* penis? It didn't seem totally out of the question...

That night I hardly slept a wink, for there seemed to be something trapped inside my stomach. Something that desperately wanted to get out. Around 3 a.m., I staggered out of my tent and liberated it. Whereupon I imagined a furry creature suddenly rising from the ground and fluttering off into the night.

Something Wild

FROM THE MOMENT I ARRIVED in Atlin, an old gold-mining town in northwestern British Columbia, I found myself staring out at Teresa Island.

Nobody I met in Atlin knew much about the island. I did hear a few stories, like the one about the two Indians who froze to death and had to be chopped up before they could be hauled to the mainland in a dogsled. But these stories didn't seem like actual events so much as typical northern tall tales.

Even the island's name was a mystery. I checked both local cemeteries and found some rather unusual inscriptions, like, for example, "Died From Gunshot Wounds, Mistaken for a Bear," but I didn't find a grave for anyone named Teresa.

The more I stared, the more curious I became about this vertiginous heap of rock and boreal forest, which—rising 4,567 feet above the lake level—is reputedly the highest inland island in the world. So when a friend in Atlin, Wayne Merry, suggested a trip to Teresa Island, I jumped at his offer. Wayne nearly jumped at his own offer, since he had long wanted to do some exploring on the island himself.

We crossed the lake in Wayne's motorboat and nosed around Teresa Island's spruce-clad eastern shore. Our first landfall was on a beach so strewn with bear scat that I wondered if local bruins had specifically designated it as a lavatory.

At a place called Twelve Mile, we stopped at a dilapidated trapper's cabin, the only house on the island. On the inside wall, some wag had posted a sheet of paper with the following "rules:" "Checkout time: 5 A.M.," "Rate: 15 Squirrel Hides," and "No Eating Popcorn in Bed."

The relatively flat southern part of the island prompted us to do some bushwhacking into the interior. At a beaver pond, we saw a huge bull moose; it gazed at us like it had never seen our species before. Later we came to a sky-blue lake totally devoid of any sign of human incursion...not even rusty fishhooks on its shore.

Still, I wasn't satisfied. There seemed to be something not quite right about reconnoitering the highest inland island in the world at such mundane altitudes. Better, much better to plant my feet on Teresa's snow-encased summit. And in Atlin I found just the person to take me to that summit: an Austrian mountaineer-artist named Gernot Dick.

Gernot chose a route that followed a steep avalanche chute on the northwest side. This route would not only keep us out of the island's virtually impenetrable forests, but it would also give us an opportunity for an advance sighting of any bear with an attitude problem.

Our initial ascent took us through what a bear might have regarded as an *al fresco* restaurant—a dense growth of raspberry bushes. Higher up, we found ourselves walking on top of an entire forest of lodgepole pines felled by an avalanche. The footing was very precarious. A single false step could mean a sprained ankle or a downhill tumble.

Gernot, who was nearly seventy, sprinted over the recumbent trees with the aplomb of a mountain goat. "Think of each step as empowerment," he called back to me.

"If this is empowerment," I yelled up at him, "then I'm against it."

We now headed up a streambed created by the summit snowfield. Occasional patches of ice sent me skidding and sliding backwards, sideways, and into the icy waters of the stream itself. Only the promise of the summit kept me from being overcome by stark raving pique.

A waterfall blocked our progress, so we climbed a ridge and scrambled over more downed trees. Gernot unsheathed his machete and cut away some of the more recalcitrant branches.

He preferred the island in the winter, he told me, because you can ski or snowshoe on top of this sort of debris. He mentioned the time he was skiing around the island and a pack of wolves seemingly in attack mode surrounded him. They seemed to think he was a caribou, albeit a weirdly shod one. They backed off at the last moment, maybe realizing that he was just a weirdly shod human being.

At one point, we were actually crawling over the downed trees on our hands and knees, then at last, long last, we were above treeline and hiking up a slope that stood at an almost vertical tilt with the rest of existence.

After an hour or two, we stopped to rest, and as Gernot played a medley of Tyrolean mountain songs on his harmonica, I gazed out on the world.

Several thousand feet below us, Atlin Lake was an expanse of turquoise that suggested the Mediterranean rather than the Canadian North. Cumulous clouds sailed by overhead like a fleet of luminous cauliflowers. The summit itself was a glistening white dome whose whiteness surpassed any other whiteness I'd ever seen.

I felt like turning a somersault, a recurring temptation, sometimes given into, when the beauty of a place goes to my head. On this incline, a somersault wouldn't have been a particularly good idea, so I just sat there, gazing. At last I told Gernot that I'd like to begin the descent.

"You're not interested in the summit?" he said, a look of astonishment on his face.

I shook my head. For I couldn't imagine the summit, any summit, being as wondrous as the place where I was now sitting. Also, I had the distinct feeling that the island wanted to be alone now—alone with its trees both fallen and unfallen, alone with its wolves, its bears, its caribou, and its moose. I felt it wanted to be alone with the absence of my species, too.

And so we started down.

Mush Rush

To MISQUOTE ROBERT SERVICE, strange things are done in the midnight sun by the men who moil for mushrooms. One such man told me that he always picks in the nude because it's easier to wash the charcoal off your skin than off your clothes; another typically picks for forty-eight hours nonstop; and yet another says he can tell when he's close to a good site because he gets what he calls "a mush rush."

Such pickers talk about the mushroom in question—the morel—in much the same way that old-time prospectors used to talk about gold, using phrases like "motherlode" and "a real bonanza" to describe their quarry. This isn't surprising, because in a good year a pound of dried morels will bring $100 or more on the European market. Once they've been rehydrated, they will grace a meal in a five-star French or German restaurant...a meal whose diners are experiencing their own slightly different version of a mush rush.

That expensive dish owes its existence to, in all probability, global warming. Due to increasingly hot, dry weather, wildfires are now burning thousands of square miles of boreal forest each year. "Burn, baby, burn" might be a picker's motto, since forest fires accelerate the growth of morels. The reason is not exactly clear. Something about fire-related nutrients or perhaps a dearth of ordinary nutrients inspires the mycelium (the mushroom's vegetative portion) to send up biblical numbers of fruiting bodies, which in turn inspire a biblical number of pickers to show up at the burn site the following year.

I visited Dawson City in the Yukon the year after 11,000 square miles of forest burned down. Outside Dawson, on the Klondike Highway, there were depots with signs advertising "Top $ for Mushrooms." Late in the day, pickers would drop by these depots with baskets of their bounty. Before you see these pickers, you can smell their aroma, a pungent amalgam of burnt forest, sweat, bug dope, and mushrooms.

Some of the pickers have tales of woe to tell. One woman lost her glasses, after which, she said, "I did my picking by Braille." The Braille method didn't seem to impress the buyer, a man who went by the sobriquet of Psycho Pete. He found a number of "blowouts" (mashed, soggy, or otherwise worthless specimens) in the woman's basket and flung them against the wall of his drying shed. "We call these ammo," he tells me.

But many of the pickers were doing extremely well. Buyers are paying $6 a pound for "wet" (fresh) specimens, and at a depot near Dawson a soot-covered man sporting a ponytail had just pocketed $965—not bad for eight hours of picking. When I asked him where he found his mushrooms, he faked an Indian accent, saying, "No Tell'um Creek."

Such reticence isn't surprising. Just as in the gold rush days, where no miner in his right mind would reveal the whereabouts of his claim, a morel picker regards everyone as a potential raider of his burn site. And just as in gold rush days, nobody seems to use their actual name. If you hang around the buying depots, sooner or later you'll run into pickers named Ivan the Terrible, Nancy the Pig, Bug-eye Bob, and Captain Ahab. One remarkably disheveled picker, who calls himself Grizzly Spasms, told me:

"Outlaws never give their real names. Let's say you're on the run or wanted for child support. This is the only job you can get. You don't need papers, a driver's license, or a credit card. It's cash up front, no questions asked. Best of all, you don't pay taxes 'cause nobody knows how much you've made...and, of course, nobody knows your real name."

Everywhere I went, I saw vehicles almost as disheveled as the pickers rattling on around local roads. One picker who wasn't rattling around was a lanky fortyish man named Doug. He had a car, but he left it at home, "because you lose more than you gain by pounding the shit out of your car on these damn roads." He hitchhiked to the Yukon from Squamish, just north of Vancouver, and when he arrived, he had only $3.80 in his pocket. Four days later, he had almost $2,000.

Camped in a lonely spot off North Fork Road, Doug didn't seem to mind my company, especially since I promised to share my mushroom bounty with him. He pulled out his map and pointed to a burn site on the Stewart Plateau several miles away. We started hiking. It was eleven o'clock at night, an excellent time to search for morels in the Yukon—there aren't any mosquitoes, and the midnight sun provides all the necessary light.

At the edge of the burn was an almost impenetrable jumble of downed trees, brambles, and underbrush. Doug hacked through the more difficult sections with an axe. In the easier sections, the only morels were "cheerios"—hollow stems that indicate a fellow forager has been here first.

Suddenly he exclaimed: "Look! There's a nice blonde..." He wasn't referring to an attractive female picker, but a light-colored morel rising from the blackened earth. A few feet away was another. Then another. And another. Doug seemed to be in a beatific state, cutting off each mushroom at the stem and placing it in his basket. An hour later, he was still more or less in the same place, hunched over a batch of darker morels, called "greens." He had two baskets; the first was already full. He was also completely covered with charcoal.

Could this large fruiting be the proverbial motherlode so eagerly sought by pickers? I asked him.

"I'll let you know after I visit Psycho Pete."

As he was picking, Doug admitted that he could probably make more money if he dried his morels and trucked them to Vancouver himself, or if he joined one of the teams being helicoptered to remote burn sites. But if he did this, he would no longer be his own boss.

"Right now I'm dancing to my own tune," he said. "I can set up my own schedule, go to sleep and wake up when I want, pick when I want. I'd rather make less money and be happy than be rolling in it and have ulcers."

The grin on his face indicated that he had in fact found the motherlode, and that it doesn't consist entirely of mushrooms.

Dangling Man

DESPITE THE SEEMINGLY RELENTLESS efforts of developers, certain parts of the Caribbean still offer the visitor a window on a remarkably natural realm. A decade or so ago, I looked through that window, indeed crashed through it, on a hike to Dominica's Boiling Lake.

Dominica, not to be confused with the Dominican Republic, is a large, surprisingly wild island in the Lesser Antilles. The capital, Roseau, has a public bathhouse in the middle of a cemetery. But the island's backcountry, as I would soon discover, is no less surreal than this extremely curious example of town planning.

I undertook the hike to the Boiling Lake during the rainy season, a time when the up-and-down trail was a quagmire of mud and slippery fronds. One false step would send me catapulting down a very steep slope, so I was very careful with my steps.

After several hours, I arrived in a valley so sulphureous and desolate that it reminded me of Iceland. At the end of this valley was a flooded fumarole through which gases from molten lava inside the earth escaped into the air. That fumarole was the Boiling Lake itself. The pressure from those gases causes it to seethe like an enormous jacuzzi, turning it sometimes black, sometimes grey, and sometimes even blue. If you put an egg in the lake, it will cook in less than three minutes.

What a weird and wonderful place, I exclaimed to myself.

I wasn't the first person to have this reaction. The Boiling Lake was discovered as recently as 1870 by a district magistrate named Edmund Watt. Mr. Watt reputedly was so astounded by his discovery that he wandered around in circles for three whole days.

On my return hike, I did the very thing I had tried so hard not to do before—I took a false step. Specifically, I slipped on a wet frond and went flying through the air. Only by grabbing an exposed tree-root did I keep myself from tumbling down the slope.

That's the good news. Now for the bad news: I was dangling more or less in mid-air, with a lush subtropical jungle fifty or so feet below me. No matter how hard I tried, I couldn't secure any sort of foothold on the muddy slope only a few inches away from me.

As I dangled there, I recalled the meeting I'd had earlier in the day with a Carib man, Jean-Baptiste, whose foot was distended like a balloon. He hadn't stepped on one of the prickly plants so common on Dominica, he told me. Rather, his girlfriend was a sorceress, and she'd cursed him with a "big foot" because he'd gone back on his promise to marry her.

At that moment, I would have gladly changed positions with Jean-Baptiste. For I was beginning to wonder how long I could continue to hold onto the root until I lost my grip and plunged down, down, down to the verdure below. In such a verdure, no team of rescuers would ever find even an insect-scavenged remnant of me. By comparison, a distended foot seemed absolutely delightful.

As it happened, my number wasn't up just yet. By putting one hand just above the other on the root and at the same time using some rodent burrows I hadn't previously noticed as footholds, I succeeded in clambering back onto firm land. But then I slipped again. This time I fell right onto the trail, with my face an inch or two from a bolus of dung left by, presumably, one of the aforementioned rodents. Could some local deity be reminding me of my helpmate?

For the rest of the hike, I didn't slip or fall, although I did come close to tripping over a large *crapaud* (frog). These amphibians are so large, in fact, that they've been known to clog up public water outlets in Roseau. This particular one was so well camouflaged that I didn't see it until the very last moment.

That evening I considered the virtues of dangling from a hillside in the Caribbean. For one thing, you can learn a lot about your mortality. For another, it's a better, albeit slightly more risky form of aerobic exercise than riding a stationary bicycle: rather than pressing on pedals and going nowhere, you're endlessly trying to get a foothold and going nowhere.

Most important of all, perhaps, you're getting up close and personal with a particular patch of earth. Years later, I feel like I had something akin to an intimate relationship with a patch of earth near Dominica's Boiling Lake. Its fibrous, gourdlike, and pleasantly rotting scent was so memorable that I can smell it this very moment, as I write these words.

Travels in Prehistory

CERTAIN PARTS OF NOVA SCOTIA are remarkably backward even for Canada's famously backward Maritime Provinces. Take Parrsboro, for example. Its cliffs instantly transport you back to the Jurassic Age. Those cliffs, a local man named Eldon George told me, are "an excellent drag site." This didn't mean that they were a hangout for men who liked to dress up like women, but that they contained numerous fossilized prints and drag marks of prehistoric creatures.

To prove his point, Eldon, a dedicated amateur fossil collector, showed me the print of a horseshoe crab, albeit a horseshoe crab that would have been only a few inches long. The drag marks of its spiky tail swiveled behind the print like a miniature S.

"Maybe 250 million years ago, these little buggers were walking around the sea bottom here—imagine!" Eldon exclaimed.

Indeed, little buggers were once a dominant form of life in these parts. In 1984, Eldon discovered a rock crisscrossed by tiny trackways at nearby Wasson Bluff. It turned out that these trackways had been made by the smallest dinosaur ever found, a creature scarcely bigger than a house sparrow. Eldon said he was more exhilarated by his discovery than if he had found the jawbone of a *T. rex*.

At one point, he showed me some small depressions in the rock and said they'd been made by pellets of ancient hail. At another point, he indicated the probable drag mark from the tail of a *Batrachopus*, a crocodilean so small that a mere toddler could have wrestled it into submission.

"I'm so lucky to be living in a storehouse for all these treasures," he observed.

We could have searched this storehouse all day, but the notorious Bay of Fundy tide was coming in, and to avoid being swallowed up by it, we headed back to Eldon's house. There he showed me one of his favorite fossils—a chunk of rock with the tracks of two copulating horseshoe crabs imbedded in it. We both agreed that it would be nice to be memorialized in this fashion.

After I left Parrsboro, I headed north along the Fundy coast and even farther back in time, to Joggins (Micmac for "Place of the Fish Weirs"). The town reminded me of the half-derelict town in Larry McMurtry's novel *The Last Picture Show*, with Fundy fog replacing West Texas dust.

At the Joggins Fossil Centre, I met Don Reid, another dedicated amateur. He showed me a fossil tree trunk and asked me to smell it. I smelled charcoal from (imagine!) a three hundred million-year-old fire probably sparked by the abundance of oxygen in the air.

"Welcome to the Carboniferous Period," Don said.

With fossils, it's not always easy to tell the players without a program, so I was fortunate that Dr. John Calder, a geologist specializing in the Carboniferous, was currently visiting Joggins. Soon he and I—joined by a couple of tourists from Toronto—were taking a prehistoric stroll along the rocky beach just below town.

Right away he pointed to a section of a fossilized tree trunk in the cliff face. Two feet in diameter and bamboo-like, it looked somewhat familiar.

"It's a *Calamites*," John said, "an ancestor of our present-day horsetail."

There happened to be a clump of horsetails growing at the edge of a nearby sward. They were hardly more than a foot high, whereas the *Calamites* would have been fifty feet high or more. This prompted one of the tourists to say, "Honey, I shrunk the horsetail."

What shrunk the horsetail, in fact, was climate change. It prospered in the hot, humid climate of the Carboniferous, but didn't do well when temperatures cooled. Yet if the current warming trend continues, perhaps the horsetail will again rise to stately heights.

John also showed us a diamond-shaped pattern in the rock, saying that it was from the stump of a *Lepidendron*, an arboreal ancestor of club moss. Once again, the ancestor would have dwarfed its descendant twenty or thirty times over.

I noticed a strange meandering pattern on an algae-covered rock at the base of the cliff. "Look—the trackway of an ancient worm!" I declared.

"Actually, it's a periwinkle's trackway from a couple of hours ago," John said, adding, "but you're not the first person to make that mistake."

Later he showed up a trackway that looked not unlike the tread marks of a Caterpillar tractor. It had been made by an ancient arthropod known as an *Arthropleura*. Similar to a millipede, the *Arthropleura* was the largest land creature in Joggins 300,000,000 years ago.

One of the tourists, a teenage girl, asked how big it might have been.

"Maybe two or three meters long," John said.

"A three-meter millipede—gross!" yelped the girl.

I thought about posing this question to her: which is more gross, a large arthropod whose specialty (probably then as now) would have been recycling the litter in its environment or a certain modern hominid whose specialty is spreading litter all over its environment?

The next day I decided to investigate the fossil cliffs by myself, so I went down to the beach and immediately found myself engulfed in a typically dense Fundy fog. I could hardly make out the cliffs, but I did see what looked like the newly exposed trunk of a *Lepidendron*.

All at once I heard a voice in the fog, and then a wraith seemed to materialize out of nowhere. The wraith turned out to be a man talking loudly into his cellphone. He was so intent on his conversation that he didn't seem to notice me...or the *Lepidendron*. A moment later, he disappeared, although I could still hear his disembodied voice shouting in the fog.

Welcome to the present age, I thought to myself.

I, Sky Burster

It was the rainy season in Western Samoa, and yet I hadn't encountered any rain at all, only the bright South Pacific sun, an orb that had much the same effect as a blast furnace. Even Samoans were bothered by the heat. They'd spend long hours submerged in the sea, their brown heads like flotillas of coconuts rising and sinking with each wave.

Then one day the sky clouded over. And as if to compensate for the previous lack of moisture, a mighty grist of rain began clamoring down from the sky. I took refuge under an empty *fale*, opened my notebook and wrote: "The monsoons have arrived with a locomotive roar."

Locomotive roar? A wholly inappropriate word, I thought, for a place so resolutely traditional, likewise a place that had never seen a train. So I crossed out "locomotive" and wrote "monumental." No good, either. For my notes already abounded with that word, usually to describe the Samoan physique—male and female, young and old, nearly every Samoan I'd met seemed to be built along the lines of an NFL linebacker.

Now I rewrote the sentence: "A tropical downpour has put Samoa in a rare Conradian mood." I crossed out rare, because I planned to use that word to describe the *manumea* (*Didunculus strigirorostris*), a quite rare bird whose taxonomic position is unclear. Could it be the last living relation of the dodo? The American naturalist Titian Peale thought so, while others have put this tooth-billed, purple-headed avian somewhere on the periphery of the pigeon family.

A short while later, I noticed a young girl had joined me in the *fale*. Swathed in a paisley-patterned lavalava, she was gazing at me with wide, intent eyes.

"What you do with paper?" she asked. At the time, I was describing a "shifting of bones" I'd recently attended. This is a ceremony where an ancestor's bones are dug up and placed on an empty seat at the dinner table. "A ghoulish custom," I wrote. But then I crossed out "ghoulish." After all, the point of the ceremony was to show the deceased that his relations were still thinking of him or her.

"I'm writing up the day's adventures," I told the girl.

"But why you tear up day's adventures?"

"Because I can't seem to find the right words. Maybe they've been swept away by all this rain..."

"Hah. You funny *palagi*. Are you married? Have husband?"

"No. And I don't have a wife, either."

By now, virtually every child for miles around had joined us in the *fale*. They touched me, examined my effects, even looked at the torn-up scraps from my notebook as if they were studying the fragments of a long-lost palimpsest. All the while, they kept shouting: "*Palagi! Palagi!*"

I averaged thirty or forty *palagi*s a day, more in remote villages, fewer in Apia, Western Samoa's capital. The word means Sky Burster and comes from the fact that the first foreigners to fetch up on these shores seemed to have burst forth from the sky itself. I confess that I liked being called a *palagi*—the word made me feel instantly transcendental, as if I was a superior or at least a super-terrestrial being.

I would often shout back at the *palagi*-hurlers: "Sacred Chicken! Sacred Chicken!" For Samoa's name (*sa*: sacred, *moa*: chicken) memorializes a pair of chickens owned by Lu, son-in-law of the god Tagaloa, creator of all things. As it happened, the birds were eaten by mistake. Their memory now lives on to this day on every map of the world.

So there I sat, a transient from the upper atmosphere, until the rain passed. Then the children left me to my scribbling. It hardly mattered that one of them, so sweet, so innocent, had picked my pocket. After all, he or she only took the balloons that I was planning to hand out anyway.

And later in the afternoon this theft granted me a vision: a solitary blue balloon moving slowly with the wind, past a stretch of greensward, past a row of thatched *fales*, past the bobbing heads of Samoans in the sea, and then venturing out to the ordinary world beyond.

How I Didn't Lose
My Head in Borneo

BORNEO'S IBAN TRIBESMEN once had a reputation for being the world's most accomplished headhunters. A poisoned arrow would whisk silently through the air. Its victim would feel like he'd been bitten by an insect, but then his breathing would be paralyzed, and he'd fall to the ground. A single stroke from an Iban parang would deliver the coup de grâce, neatly separating the head from his body.

I wanted to meet some real-life headhunters (where I live, there's only the debased corporate variety), so, finding myself in Borneo, I boarded a motorized dugout canoe and traveled down a series of increasingly remote jungle rivers until I came to an Iban longhouse.

Soon I was seated on a mat next to the chief, a man who was embellished with such a circuitry of blue-black tatoos that he looked like a giant thumbprint. Dangling from the rafters directly above us was a rattan bag of skulls belonging to former members of the Japanese Imperial Army; they'd been taken during World War II during the so-called "Ten Bob a Knob" program, whereby the Iban got ten shillings for each Japanese head they brought in.

The Japanese "knobs" were more than sixty years old. I asked the chief whether anyone in the longhouse still whipped off the occasional head. My guide, a Malay named Bakhri, translated his answer.

"The Iban don't take heads anymore," the chief said.

"Not even to stay in practice?"

He shook his head. In his father's day, he said, the most popular guy with the girls was the one who took the most heads. If you didn't participate in headhunting raids, you'd probably remain a bachelor. But nowadays there were less bloodthirsty ways to get ahead (so to speak) with a woman. A young man might go to work in the oilfields of Brunei, for instance. He would then bring back a sewing machine, and that would please a woman just as much as a human head might have pleased her in the old days.

I asked a young woman sitting near me which she would prefer, a sewing machine or a nice fresh human head. She chose the sewing machine. But the chief thought I had something other than a scholarly interest in the subject, because he asked me if I was married.

"No," I told him.

"You would like a wife, maybe?" he said.

Before I could answer, a girl who couldn't have been more than sixteen was ushered forth for my inspection. She was slender, delicate-featured, and with silky black hair cascading almost to her waist. She caught my gaze and returned it with a flirtatious gaze of her own.

"I'm at least three times her age," I told the chief.

"A person's age doesn't matter to us," he replied. "What matters to us is his character."

Lovely though the girl was, I figured I'd be spending the rest of my days here if I married her, so I told the chief that marriage was a big deal where I came from, and that I needed a bit of time to think it over.

Bakhri now leaned over to me and whispered that our hosts might be offended if I turned down the girl, and while they had given up headhunting, my refusal might force them to take it up again. He grinned and drew an imaginary parang across his (i.e., my) throat.

That night I lay down on the longhouse verandah. The humidity was at least 110%; at first my bones felt like they were turning to butter, then they felt like they were melting. Every time I fell into a fitful sleep, something would wake me up—a dog barking, a cock crowing, or a pig rooting around noisily under the longhouse. Meanwhile, the cicadas in the surrounding jungle were like an orchestra of chainsaws.

A yellow, doubtless flea-ridden mutt kept nudging up against me, and I kept pushing it away. Once, when I'd actually fallen asleep, it nudged me again, and—my temper now stretched to the limit—I gave it a strong kick. I heard a very undoglike scream. For I'd kicked my "wife," who had crawled under my mosquito net to (I figured) consummate our union.

What to do? I could hardly apologize to the girl because we didn't have a single word in common; and even if we had, she might not have appreciated being told that I thought she was a dog. So I grabbed her arms and gazed apologetically into her eyes. Well, I thought I was gazing apologetically, but she seemed to think I was gazing amorously, because she wriggled out of her sarong.

Now I was in a real predicament. If I responded to the girl, would she think I was consenting to the marriage? And if I didn't, would she feel rejected? I didn't want to lose my head over a woman, at least not literally. In my confusion, I found myself at once fondling the girl and pushing her away. At last I made a gesture that would have been unmistakable in any language: Go away.

The girl gave me a perplexed look, then put on her sarong and slipped away. I felt miserable—for both of us. Also, I still didn't know if I had offended local proprieties, with the result that every creak in the longhouse became an Iban warrior edging toward me and wielding a parang. Needless to say, I didn't get any more sleep that night.

The next morning Bakhri and I were back on the river, and I told him about my nocturnal visitor. He, too, looked perplexed. "Why you no make sex with girl?" he asked.

"Because I didn't want my head to end up in the longhouse rafters…"

"Oh no. Iban very polite people, offer you girl for the night. Old, old custom. They would not put your head in rafters."

"But you said…"

"I tell joke. You know joke? I don't know word in English for it."

I was not amused. In fact, I thought about knocking him out of the canoe. For I knew that I would never find people anywhere else in the wide, wide world who were as polite to their guests as my ex-headhunting hosts.

The Incidental Traveler

THE STORY GOES THAT Jules Verne once paid a visit to the French Foreign Secretary. After he identified himself to the Secretary's clerk, the man leaped up, dusted off a chair, and said: "Please sit down, Monsieur Verne. You must be exhausted from all your travels..."

In truth, Jules Verne—author of 103 volumes known collectively as *Voyages Extraordinaires*—traveled rather less than most of us. He never circumnavigated the globe like Phileas Fogg, the hero of *Around the World in Eighty Days*. He never went to the Arctic (where I've been many times), the South Pacific (where I've been a dozen times), or Asia (where I've been five times). He spent just one week in North America, where he saw nothing more extraordinary than Lake Erie in the process of freezing over.

Verne's favorite pastime was hardly adventurous—he liked to cruise along the French coast in his yacht *St. Michel*. But he almost never looked at anything other than the pad of paper on which he was writing with his goose quill pen.

His wife Honorine once remarked: "How can you write such beautiful things, Jules, when you gaze at the world with your buttocks?"

This was the same man who opened up the sky for future travelers. The rocket scientist Werner von Braun claimed Verne as his major inspiration. I attribute my own desire to venture off the map to the fact that I read Verne's *The Mysterious Island* at an impressionable age. Even as I write the words of that title, I feel an urge to search the planet until I've found an island that has fallen off it.

An injury—among the most bizarre since Hannibal lost an eye trying to count his elephants in the Alps—put an end even to Verne's modest trip-taking. His deranged nephew Gaston shot him in the foot. Gaston thought this action would call attention to Uncle Jules's genius and thus gain him a seat in the prestigious French Academy.

Gaston's strategy failed, and Verne walked with difficulty for the rest of his life. Meanwhile, the French Academy continued to elect authors who wrote in classical quatrains rather than one who seemingly had intimate dealings with giant squids.

Verne's sedate notion of travel may have been the consequence of a childhood promise. At the age of eleven, he bribed a cabin boy to give up his berth on the three-masted schooner *Coralie*, bound for the West Indies, but his father caught wind of the plan. Scolded and birched, young Jules promised his family that he would only travel in his imagination from now on.

As if to compensate for any actual travels, that imagination whisked Verne off to our lunar neighbor a century before the Apollo mission. It transported him to the North Pole forty-five years before Peary may or may not have reached it, and to the South Pole forty-one years before Amundsen.

Likewise, his imagination invented movies, submarines, helicopters, guided missiles, TVs, air conditioners, and condensed food, not to mention a computer-like device very similar to the one which I'm using at the moment.

Around the World in Eighty Days was his greatest commercial success. It was serialized before book publication, and readers laid bets for or against Phileas Fogg. A cruise line representative offered Verne a staggering sum if only he would bring Fogg home safely on one of his line's steamships. But Verne would not allow advertising to beggar his craft.

It has become almost a commonplace to say that the predictions in Verne's novels have all come true. Ironically, *Around the World in Eighty Days* is one of the few Jules Verne works whose predictions have not come true. That's because hardly anyone journeys around the world in eighty days anymore. For jetting to a destination is quicker as well as more convenient than taking a balloon or an elephant to get there.

Even so, Verne may have hit upon a perfect pace for the dedicated traveler: Slow down, seek out carriages and sledges, maybe even hop a pachyderm or two. You might witness some extraordinary things...

Local Bird Makes Good

ON MAY 23, 1833, John James Audubon, traveling on the U.S. revenue-cutter *Swiftsure*, landed on New Brunswick's White Head Island to look for a certain bird. Not so long ago, I visited the same island to look for the same bird.

Shortly after the ferry from Grand Manan docked, a man in a geriatric pickup offered me a lift. He also offered me some dulse, an edible seaweed commonly harvested in this part of the Bay of Fundy. At the slightest provocation, locals will reach for their bags of dulse and crunch away on the dried contents.

I started telling the driver about Audubon and his visit to the island, but he interrupted me. Audubon, he said, had stayed with his cousin, William Frankland, and according to family lore, the Franklands had run out of salt, so the artist-naturalist cheerfully sprinkled gunpowder on his food (the eminent Victorian Francis Galton also considered gunpowder an excellent substitute for salt).

"Anything else your family say about him?" I asked.

"Well, I heard that he liked to eat old wives' eggs."
"Old wife" is a euphemism for the bird both Audubon and I had come here to see.

Up and down the East Coast, everyone else liked the eggs too, which is one reason why the bird's numbers had undergone a serious decline in Audubon's day. Another reason: its feathers were popular adornments on women's hats; so popular, in fact, that ornithologist Frank Chapman—creator of the Audubon Christmas Bird Count—once titled a lecture "Women as an Enemy of Birds."

As we were driving along the 1,250-acre island's only road, I noticed a number of boarded-up houses. The driver said that they belonged to Americans who came here only for a week or two in the summer. He was not pleased to see his island turning into a playground for outsiders.

"Those houses were once owned by fishermen," he told me. "Now they're owned by folks who just want property by the sea. What's happening is that we islanders are becoming an endangered species ourselves..."

My host dropped me off at the site of William Frankland's house. It was in the woods behind this house that Audubon made an astonishing discovery: the bird he wanted to see, previously a ground nester, was now building nests in fir trees in order to escape the depredations of humans. Some of these nests were as much as forty feet off the ground, thus showing the adaptability of the bird in question.

"How strangely Nature has provided them with the means of securing their eggs and young from their arch-enemy Man," wrote Audubon. No one had devoted much attention to the bird before him. In fact, the portrait he painted of it while he was on White Island was the first ever done by a professional artist.

I wondered if a few birds might still be nesting in trees here. So I began hiking through the woods, studying every fir I saw. The only nest I saw belonged to a red squirrel, which, upon seeing me, proceeded to raise an unholy racket.

I continued walking. The ground was littered with rusty beer cans, Vienna sausage tins, and scraps of plastic, ample evidence that I was not the first person since Audubon to pass this way. In a short time, I saw a robin, a ruby-crowned kinglet, a white-throated sparrow, and a boreal chickadee, none of which was the bird I was looking for.

At last I emerged from the woods and came out at the edge of a marsh known locally as Grandma's Heath. Seeing a grove of firs a few hundred feet away, I began crossing the marsh. Soon I found myself sinking into sphagnum muck. When I tried to walk to the nearest elevated land, I only ended up deeper in the muck, which seemed eager to swallow me up, rucksack and all.

I cursed Grandma, whoever she was. Her heath made King Lear's "blasted heath" seem like a putting green.

By the time I reached dry ground, I had so much of the heath clinging to me that I probably looked more like a habitat than a person. A couple of kids stopped playing ball and stared at me as if I'd just arrived from a distant galaxy.

I found a path leading down to the sea and, stooping over, I started washing off bits of the heath. Suddenly I looked up. There, in the water, were at least a hundred of the birds I'd been searching for. Several hundred more seemed to have colonized an offshore islet. There were even a few on a nearby ledge, gazing at me warily.

The bird had made a remarkable comeback since the time Audubon passed this way. You can now find it almost everywhere on the North American continent. That some people consider it virtually a pest is a tribute to its ability to adapt to settings as dissimilar as an urban dump and a fir tree on a small Atlantic island.

The bird is, of course, the herring gull.

The Green Man

THE NUNAVIK VILLAGE of Kangiqsujuaq does not seem like a particularly superstitious place, but if you mention the petroglyphs on Qajartalik Island to the local Inuit, you'll probably get some rather fearful looks. For they believe that these incised faces, known locally as "devil masks," are evil—powerfully evil. If you want to visit the island, you do so at your own peril, they'll tell you.

Well, not all of them will tell you that. I met a fiftyish Inuk named Yakaga who didn't appear to be at all afraid of the petroglyphs. He knew that they'd been carved by the so-called Dorset people a thousand or more years ago, and that they were probably of shamanic origin. The only evil spirits on Qajartalik, he told me, were mosquitoes. And, yes, he'd be willing to take me to the island the next day.

So it was that we piled several days' worth of provisions into his twenty-two-foot freighter canoe and headed into Hudson Strait. A strong lateral swell rocked the boat, but we still made good progress. We passed islands with ancient kayak stands near the shore and other islands that seemed to be composed exclusively of Canadian Shield granite. Yakaga pointed to one of these latter islands and said its name in Inuktitut means "not enough moss there to wipe your ass with."

Qajartalik was forty or so miles from Kangiqsujuaq, and we got there by early evening. As we approached the island, the odor of putrefaction assailed our nostrils. An olfactory warning from the evil spirits? Not at all. The smell emanated from a rotting beluga whale stretched out on the shingle beach. Three polar bears were engaged in a culinary orgy on its carcass. One of the bears gazed at us with an icy stare that said "Stay away..."

"Not a good idea to camp here tonight," Yakaga said.

Needless to say, I agreed with him.

He knew of an abandoned cabin several miles away, on the Ivartoq Peninsula. We decided to spend the night there and visit the petroglyphs the following day.

The cabin turned out to be little more than four sagging walls and a perforated tarpaper roof, but at least it offered more protection from a marauding bear than a tent. After a supper of caribou stew, we unrolled our sleeping bags on the dirt floor. I fell asleep to the vapors of my sweaty polypro and the clatter of mosquitoes on the cabin's lone opaque window.

After maybe an hour, I was awakened by the loudest snoring I'd ever heard. Actually, it sounded more like a donkey braying into a microphone than a person snoring. Every once in a while, the pitch would become higher, as if the donkey had ingested an orchestra of flutes, but the decibel level remained the same.

Neither ear plugs or burying my head in my pillow did any good, so I nudged Yakaga. There was no response, so I shouted: "Yakaga, turn over! Your snoring is driving me crazy..." He woke up, looked at me quizzically, mumbled something in Inuktitut, and then went back to sleep. The snoring came back with a vengeance, and I slept fitfully for the rest of the night.

The next morning we were loading the boat when Yakaga announced: "We're going back to Kangiqsujuaq now."

The look on his face told me that he was serious. I was dumbfounded. "Because of what I said about your snoring?" I asked.

He nodded and continued to pack the boat.

I didn't believe him. He's afraid of the devil masks, I thought, and he doesn't want to admit it to me. So I said in what I thought was a comforting voice, "Don't worry, those petroglyphs won't hurt you."

"We're going back to Kangiqsujuaq," he repeated, this time with considerable emphasis.

To say that I was disappointed would be an understatement—I was pretty damn upset. My eyes scanned the rock-ribbed shoreline (might there be some petroglyphs here?), and I noticed several old burial cairns on a rise perhaps five hundred feet from where we'd parked the boat.

"I have to answer Nature's call before we go," I told Yakaga, then wandered over to the nearest of the cairns.

Inuit burial cairns of a certain vintage tend to be surprisingly large; this one was no exception. It seemed to be about four feet high, five feet wide, and eight feet long. Why so large? "The dead need lots of breathing room," an Inuit elder on Baffin Island once explained to me, adding that a person's worldly goods used to be buried with him or her.

I peered into the small hole at the top of the cairn and saw a skull that seemed to be peering right back at me. That was all I could discern, so I stuck the lens of my camera into the hole, then activated the flash.

A more or less intact skeleton in a fetal position appeared on my LCD screen. The posture suggested that the skeleton had belonged to an Inuk of the Thule Period (roughly AD 1100 to 1700), for the Thule Inuit believed that you should leave the world in your original posture. Several spearpoints lying on the ground indicated that the cairn's occupant had been male.

But what struck me most of all was this: the skeleton was almost completely botanized.

From skull to phalanges, I saw algae, lichens, and growths of a *Tetraplodon* moss species. A green lichen (*Peltigera* species?) was growing on the skeleton's pelvis, and there was a greenish-yellow algal growth on the neck and along a few of the ribs. A patch of a different kind of moss seemed to be just starting out on the lower left leg. Not to be outdone, the rock surface inside the cairn boasted another greenish lichen, probably a *Lepraria* species.

I took a few more photographs, gazing in delight at each one. I don't think the petroglyphs on Qajartalik Island, if I had seen them, would have given me such pleasure. Ah green, I thought—what a splendid color to accompany one's journey to dust.

"That took a long time," Yakaga said when I climbed into the boat.

"You can't rush Nature," I told him, smiling.

And I smiled all the way back to Kangiqsujuaq.

Envoi: On Being Lost

I WAS SOMEWHERE in the Ecuadorian Amazon, sweating profusely and besieged by a seemingly endless relay of biting, stinging insects, one of which—the konga ant—engaged in both activities. It would affix its pincers to my skin, then curl its abdomen around and inject me with its venom. Compared to a konga ant, the mosquitoes seemed as warm and cuddly as teddy bears.

Take the trail on your right, my hosts had told me, and I followed their directions. But then I noticed a strange-looking fungus on a fallen log, and I wandered over to investigate it. When I got back, the trail had disappeared. Looking around, I failed to find it. Looking around some more, I failed to find it even more dramatically.

This was hardly the first time I'd managed to get lost. Indeed, I seem to make a practice of it and, in the process, get my fellow travelers lost, too. Once, in the Canadian Arctic, I took an Inuk to an island where I'd discovered an unusual archaeological site, but we somehow ended up on the wrong island. Closer to home, I took a documentary filmmaker into the New Hampshire woods and succeeded in getting both of us lost. This latter incident has been memorialized on film. Here I might mention that the English naturalist Thomas Nuttall found numerous new species when his sense of direction deserted him.

If a wrong turn can be made, I'll find a way, God or his absence willing, to make it; if there's a sign pointing to the right, I'll habitually go to the left; and if a compass or GPS can be misread, I'll misread it. In justifying such behavior, I can't even claim dyslexia; I can only claim incompetence.

Yet being lost, for a writer, is not necessarily a bad thing, since it can turn into a source of what's commonly known as material. You can't experience konga ants or the pitiless Amazonian sun if you're stuck in an air-conditioned hotel room. Likewise, our perpetually shrinking planet becomes a capacious place if you're lost. And if you're lost, the scenery is almost always fresh, often disturbingly so.

At least that's the way I see it now, a couple of years after my trip to Ecuador. My Shuar Indian hosts had seen it somewhat differently, though. Only a bumbling idiot, their expressions informed me, could have gotten lost en route to the community outhouse.

About the Author

LAWRENCE MILLMAN has written fifteen books, including such titles as *Our Like Will Not Be There Again*, *Last Places*, *Northern Latitudes*, *An Evening Among Headhunters*, *A Kayak Full of Ghosts*, and—most recently—the first ever guidebook to New England mushrooms. His essays and articles have appeared in *National Geographic*, *Smithsonian*, *Sports Illustrated*, *Atlantic Monthly*, and *Outside*. As a traveler, he chooses his destinations based on the Internet: if a place doesn't have a website, he'll immediately pack his bags and head there. He keeps a post office box in Cambridge, Massachusetts.